Quantum Computing - Innovations and Applications in Modern Research

Edited by Bruno Carpentieri

Published in London, United Kingdom

Quantum Computing - Innovations and Applications in Modern Research
http://dx.doi.org/10.5772/intechopen.1000362
Edited by Bruno Carpentieri

Contributors
Abdallah Slaoui, Abdelali Sajia, Alvir Nobel, Bilal Benzimoun, Bruno Carpentieri, David Levy, Dylan Kneidel, Esam El-Araby, Ishraq Ul Islam, Lalla Btissam Drissi, Manu Chaudhary, Mingyoung Jeng, Nada Ikken, Nicholas R. Allgood, Rachid Ahl Laamara, Theresa Melvin, Vinayak Jha

First published in London, United Kingdom, 2024 by IntechOpen
IntechOpen is the global imprint of INTECHOPEN LIMITED, registered in England and Wales, registration number: 11086078, 167-169 Great Portland Street, London, W1W 5PF, United Kingdom

British Library Cataloguing-in-Publication Data
A catalogue record for this book is available from the British Library

Additional hard and PDF copies can be obtained from orders@intechopen.com

Quantum Computing - Innovations and Applications in Modern Research
Edited by Bruno Carpentieri
p. cm.
Print ISBN 978-0-85466-386-6
Online ISBN 978-0-85466-385-9
eBook (PDF) ISBN 978-0-85466-387-3

For EU product safety concerns :
IN TECH d.o.o., Prolaz Marije Krucifikse Kozulić 3, 51000 Rijeka, Croatia,
info@intechopen.com or visit our website at intechopen.com.

Meet the editor

Bruno Carpentieri obtained a Laurea degree in Applied Mathematics in 1997 from Bari University, Italy. He obtained a Ph.D. in Computer Science from the Institut National Polytechnique de Toulouse (INPT), France. After a post-doctoral appointment at the Institute of Mathematics and Scientific Computing, University of Graz, Austria, and as a consultant for a European project in cardiac modeling at CRS4 in Sardinia, Italy, he served as an assistant professor at the Bernoulli Institute for Mathematics, Computer Science and Artificial Intelligence, University of Groningen, Netherlands, and as a Reader in Applied Mathematics at the School of Science and Technology, Nottingham Trent University, UK. Since 2017, Dr. Carpentieri has been an Associate Professor in Applied Mathematics at the Faculty of Computer Science, University of Bozen-Bolzano, Italy. His research interests are in the fields of applied mathematics, numerical linear algebra, and high-performance computing. He served as a member of the scientific advisory board of several conference panels in computational mathematics and high-performance scientific computing. He is an editorial board member of the *Journal of Applied Mathematics*, a review editor of *Frontiers in Applied Mathematics and Statistics*, an editorial committee member of *Mathematical Reviews* (American Mathematical Society), and a reviewer of more than thirty scientific journals in numerical analysis and scientific computing. He has supervised twenty student projects at BSc, MSc, and Ph.D. levels and is the author of more than fifty publications in peer-reviewed scientific journals.

Contents

Preface

In recent decades, the field of computer science has undergone rapid and transformative changes. The exponential growth in computational power, described by the famous Moore's Law, has driven advancements across various domains, from data processing to artificial intelligence. However, this relentless pursuit of speed and efficiency has encountered significant challenges. Physical limitations in transistor scaling, power consumption, and heat dissipation have led to decreasing returns in traditional silicon-based technologies. As we approach the end of Moore's Law, the need for new paradigms in computing has become increasingly urgent.

Parallel processing and multicore architectures have provided significant advancements, enabling computers to execute multiple tasks simultaneously. This shift has prompted innovations in software development, requiring the development of new algorithms and programming models to harness the power of parallelism effectively. Parallel computing has become fundamental in addressing a wide range of complex problems, from large-scale simulations to data-intensive tasks, revolutionizing various fields and applications. However, despite these advances, certain computational problems remain very difficult to solve or even intractable for classical computers. These include complex optimization problems like the Traveling Salesman Problem and scheduling issues, cryptographic challenges such as integer factorization and discrete logarithms, and the simulation of quantum systems in fields like chemistry and high-energy physics.

Quantum computing is an innovative technology that has the potential to completely transform the field of computational science. Unlike conventional computers that rely on bits as the smallest unit of information, quantum computers use qubits, which leverage the principles of quantum mechanics. Qubits can exist in multiple states simultaneously (superposition) and can be entangled with one another, allowing for a level of parallelism and computational power that is exponentially greater than that of classical systems.

The promise of quantum computing extends across various fields. In cryptography, quantum algorithms like Shor's algorithm threaten to break widely used encryption methods, while new quantum-resistant cryptographic techniques are being developed. In materials science and pharmaceuticals, quantum simulations could lead to breakthroughs in understanding molecular structures and interactions, paving the way for new drugs and materials. Optimization problems in finance, logistics, and artificial intelligence stand to benefit immensely from the speed and efficiency of quantum algorithms.

This volume on recent research topics in quantum computing and related technology delves into these transformative changes. The five chapters presented here explore key aspects of modern quantum computing research. Chapter 1 investigates the transformative impact of quantum computing, discussing foundational quantum mechanics concepts and attempting to provide insight into the convergence of quantum and classical computer domains. Chapter 2 explores the theoretical advancements and practical implementations of quantum gates and circuits, highlighting the transformative potential of quantum systems in computing and communication. Chapter 3 offers an overview of quantum entanglement, focusing on its mathematical foundations, manipulation, and quantification, and underscoring its significance in quantum information theory. Chapter 4 explores the challenges of error suppression in Noisy Intermediate-Scale Quantum (NISQ) systems and highlights the potential of adaptive quantum machine learning methods to advance fault-tolerant quantum computing. Chapter 5 examines adiabatic quantum computing and quantum annealing, analyzing their foundations in the adiabatic theorem and their application in solving combinatorial optimization problems. Chapter 6 reviews recent research on practical applications of quantum computing, such as dimension reduction, pattern recognition, quantum sorting, and quantum communications, highlighting optimized algorithms and practical implementations using quantum wavelet transform and Grover's algorithm.

These chapters collectively offer a comprehensive view of quantum computing's current capabilities and future directions. They highlight the interdisciplinary nature of the field, drawing on insights from physics, computer science, and engineering to overcome challenges and harness the potential of quantum technology. As we stand on the brink of this new era, the contributions in this volume reflect the evolving role of quantum computing in shaping technological advancements and scientific understanding. We hope this collection serves as a valuable resource for researchers, practitioners, and anyone interested in the future of computing. I would like to express my sincere gratitude to IntechOpen, particularly Publishing Process Manager Ms. Kristina Kardum Cvitan, whose invaluable support and expertise have been instrumental throughout the editorial process of this volume.

Bruno Carpentieri
Faculty of Engineering,
Free University of Bozen-Bolzano,
Bolzano, Italy

Chapter 1

Introductory Chapter: Transforming Computing – From Classical to Quantum Paradigms

Bruno Carpentieri

1. Introduction

The origins of computing trace back to the nineteenth century with the visionary work of Charles Babbage, who designed mechanical devices such as the difference engine and analytical engine that laid the groundwork for modern computers. During World War II, Alan Turing's breakthroughs in cryptanalysis at Bletchley Park, including the development of the Bombe machine to decrypt German Enigma codes, showcased the practical application of early computing. Post-war, the advent of electronic computers, such as the Electronic Numerical Integrator and Computer (ENIAC) in 1946, heralded the era of electronic computing. Subsequent decades witnessed the evolution of programming languages, the development of microprocessors, and the rise of personal computers, leading to today's interconnected world of the Internet and networked computing.

Over the past decades, computer science and high-performance computing have seen several major changes. At first, the focus was on making CPUs faster by increasing their clock speeds. However, by the early 2000s, this approach faced physical limits, like overheating and high power consumption. In response to the limitations of increasing CPU clock speeds, the computing industry pivoted toward multicore processors, where multiple cores work together for parallel processing. This change transformed computing, allowing computers to execute multiple tasks simultaneously. Parallel processing helps improve performance, but it also requires new software that can use multiple cores effectively. Programs have to be optimized or rewritten to effectively leverage parallelism, which introduces complexities not present in single-threaded applications. As Moore's law slows down and silicon technology reaches its limits, the future of computing depends more on innovations that enhance parallel processing and optimize performance for various tasks.

The advent of petascale computing marked a significant milestone in computational capability. Petascale systems, capable of performing at least one petaflop (10^{15} floating-point operations per second), enabled unprecedented advances in scientific research and computational modeling in fields like climate science, astrophysics, and genomics. The next big step is exascale computing, which aims to reach speeds of one exaflop (10^{18} operations per second), making it hundreds of times more powerful than today's supercomputers. These advancements could transform areas like precision medicine, energy research, and artificial intelligence by providing faster insights and more detailed simulations than ever before [1]. Achieving this, however, will require innovations in hardware to manage power, improve data handling, and ensure reliability.

2. Quantum computing: the next frontier in technology

In the evolution of computer science, from clock speed races to parallel computing and petascale architectures, quantum computing emerges as a transformative technology, representing a revolutionary departure from classical paradigms. Unlike classical systems that use bits, quantum computers use qubits, which can represent and process information using quantum mechanical phenomena like superposition and entanglement [2]. This allows quantum computers to perform certain computations exponentially more efficiently than classical machines. For example, they can factor large numbers, simulate quantum systems, and optimize complex problems far faster than classical computers. Quantum computing shows promise in fields such as cryptography, drug discovery, materials science, and optimization. Moreover, in optimization and artificial intelligence, quantum algorithms offer faster solutions to combinatorial optimization problems and have the potential to enhance machine learning capabilities, enabling more efficient data analysis and decision-making in critical areas like finance and health care. In scientific research, quantum simulations could revolutionize material science by enabling detailed modeling of molecular interactions, leading to discoveries in new materials and pharmaceuticals [3]. Quantum computers can also deepen our understanding of quantum systems and simulate complex phenomena like high-energy physics simulations more efficiently [4]. Overall, while exascale computing systems are indispensable for managing vast datasets, running large-scale simulations, and executing complex AI models, quantum computers complement this by providing efficient solutions to specialized tasks within broader computational workflows.

Despite the immense potential of quantum computing, several challenges must be addressed to realize its full capabilities [5]. One major hurdle is managing qubit coherence and reducing error rates, as quantum bits are highly susceptible to environmental noise and decoherence. Developing effective quantum error correction methods and creating algorithms that can tolerate noise is essential for practical quantum computing. Scalability is another critical issue, as current quantum systems are limited in the number of qubits they can reliably control. Additionally, the development of quantum algorithms that can leverage the unique properties of quantum mechanics for real-world applications requires extensive research and innovation [6]. Interdisciplinary collaboration between physicists, computer scientists, and engineers is crucial to overcome these obstacles.

Key aspects of modern quantum computing research include delving into fundamental concepts like quantum entanglement, teleportation, and Bell's inequalities, which are essential for quantum computing and communication. Addressing technological challenges, particularly with noisy intermediate-scale quantum (NISQ) systems and quantum error correction, underscores efforts to enhance reliability and scalability. Exploring alternative approaches such as adiabatic quantum computing (AQC) broadens perspectives on quantum computational models. Moreover, investigating practical applications demonstrates quantum computing's potential impact across industries. These areas collectively provide a comprehensive view of quantum computing's current capabilities and future directions, reflecting its evolving role in shaping technological advancements and scientific understanding.

DOI: http://dx.doi.org/10.5772/intechopen.1005918

Author details

Bruno Carpentieri
Faculty of Engineering, Free University of Bozen-Bolzano, Bolzano, Italy

*Address all correspondence to: bcarpentieri@gmail.com

References

[1] Bader DA. Petascale Computing: Algorithms and Applications. Boca Raton, Florida, United States: CRC Press; 2007

[2] Hirvensalo M. Quantum Computing. Berlin/Heidelberg, Germany: Springer Science & Business Media; 2013

[3] Bauer B, Bravyi S, Motta M, Chan GK-L. Quantum algorithms for quantum chemistry and quantum materials science. Chemical Reviews. 2020;**120**(22):12685-12717

[4] Nachman B, Provasoli D, De Jong WA, Bauer CW. Quantum algorithm for high energy physics simulations. Physical Review Letters. 2021;**126**(6):062001

[5] Almudever CG, Lao L, Fu X, Khammassi N, Ashraf I, Iorga D, et al. The engineering challenges in quantum computing. In: Design, Automation & Test in Europe Conference & Exhibition (DATE). Piscataway, New Jersey, United States: IEEE; 2017. pp. 836-845

[6] Childs AM, Van Dam W. Quantum algorithms for algebraic problems. Reviews of Modern Physics. 2010;**82**(1):1

Chapter 2

Quantum Communication Protocols: From Theory to Implementation in the Quantum Computer

Abdallah Slaoui, Nada Ikken, Lalla Btissam Drissi and Rachid Ahl Laamara

Abstract

In recent years, notable progress has been achieved in the theoretical investigation of quantum systems as computational tools. This has given rise to the development of quantum computing and quantum information, fields that delve into the feasibility of employing quantum systems for information processing objectives. Essential to the manipulation of qubits and the facilitation of quantum computations are quantum gates. Comparable to classical gates, these quantum counterparts are actions designed to alter the state of qubits. Among them are the Hadamard gate, CNOT gate, and Toffoli gate, each imbued with distinct functionalities that collectively enrich the repertoire of quantum computation tools. As we progress through this chapter, we embark on a journey that unveils the complexities of quantum communication. From the foundational concepts of quantum mechanics to the advanced realms of quantum teleportation, we have witnessed the potency of quantum entanglement to teleport quantum states. Furthermore, we have delved into the practical implementation of circuits using Qiskit, gaining a grasp of the art of orchestrating qubit operations, measurements, and corrections. Standing at the convergence of the quantum and classical realms, this chapter aims to provide a comprehensive perspective, exposing the intricate web of quantum communication and computing, while paving the way for a future in which quantum technologies redefine the boundaries of the achievable.

Keywords: quantum teleportation, quantum gates, quantum information, quantum communications, quantum computer

1. Introduction

Over the course of the previous years, the landscape of computer technology has experienced a spectacular transformation pointed out by an amazing process of decreasing. From the microprocessor that made a huge revolution in the worls, to the microchips memos that had a lot of free space to save more Data and informations.

Throughout this revolutionary journey, although the implementation of computer hardware has seen many modifications, the basic mathematical model directing computers has maintained a continuous presence [1]. Yet, on the horizon of this technological continuity. The shift to such a microscopic scale raises issues since the conventional mathematical methods used for computers could no longer work due to the significantly different conditions [2]. This addressing transformation has cleared the way for the birth of "quantum computing," indicating a considerable difference from classical computing technologies. To comprehend the transition from classical computers to quantum computers, it's vital to appreciate the basic role that boolean functions and classical gates in developing classical computing. Boolean functions and classical gates are like the building blocks of classical computers. These functions work using a binary system of 1 s and 0 s, and classical gates understand this binary input, performing computations and logical judgments. The progress of classical computing from its initial stages to the powerful computers we have today was made possible by the development of growing complex and powerful classical gates. These gates, in turn, permitted the development of complex boolean functions that serves as numerous computing processes. This advancement has its roots in the thorough optimization of classical gates, boosting the efficiency and speed of calculations. Over time, the manipulation of boolean functions using classical gates led to the creation of classical algorithms and software that have changed industries and everyday life. The journey to quantum computing builds upon this basis by acknowledging the fundamental physical nature of computing devices [3].

In the realm of computing, the advent of computers has significantly diminished the level of human effort needed to accomplish tasks. Computers come in a range of sizes, contingent upon the type, magnitude, and inherent complexity of the task at hand. With the progression of technology, the development of high-performance, high-throughput, and high-memory classical computers has become increasingly feasible. Classical computers store data in the form of binary digits, known as bits, within a memory device, where each bit represents either a "1" or a "0". All processing within classical computers adheres to the same logical framework. It's worth noting, however, that this logic-oriented approach can lead to heightened power consumption [4]. Quantum computers are the next generation of computers that solve problems using quantum theory notions. The quantum computer uses the qubit as its fundamental unit, which leverages quantum computing concepts such as superposition and entanglement, giving the qubit the efficiency of showing numerous logical states at the same time. Quantum computing is not emerging separately from traditional computing. Many design considerations for quantum computers are influenced by what is done with conventional computers [5]. Some aspects of quantum computing might seem arbitrary to those unfamiliar with traditional computing. A basic understand of classical computing facilitates comprehension of quantum computing. Many of the ideas covered in this chapter are included in the table below. Quantum computing presents a new domain of computation where the complex interactions between qubits, obtained by quantum gates, have the ability to solve some problems 10 times quicker than classical computers. While still in its new phases, quantum computing offers a fascinating area that challenges traditional concepts of computation and holds the potential of transforming areas such as encryption, optimization, and material science [6]. The shift from boolean functions and classical gates to the quantum gates represents our ever-evolving knowledge of the universe and our unceasing effort to exploit its subtleties for unprecedented technological development. In this book chapter, we will cover the classical column, beginning with bits. Then we will perform

Classical computers	Quantum computers
Bits	Qubits
Logical Gates	Unitary Gates
Boolean	Linear
Matlab, C++, C...	IBM, Qiskit, QuTech...
Vivado Simulator	Qasm, Aer, Belem Simulator

Table 1.
Comparison between classical computers and quantum computers.

computation on these bits using logical gates. The math of classical computing is boolean algebra, and we can program classical circuits using hardware description languages. In contrast we will talk about Quantum computer and how significantly can be faster than classical computers at some tasks (**Table 1**).

2. A brief review on classical computer

2.1 Boolean functions: definitions and examples

The concept of a logic gate ensue from efforts to formalize the laws of thought. Binary variables have two possible values: 0 or 1. A Boolean function is an expression that includes two binary variables, the binary operators AND and OR, one binary operator NOT, parentheses, and the equal sign. A function's value can be 0 or 1, based on the values of the variables in the Boolean function or expression. A Boolean function's inputs are typically represented by variables such as A, B, C, and so on, and the output is a logical operator-based combination of these variables [7]. These are the most often used logical operators in Boolean functions:

- AND: Denoted by the symbol ($\wedge$), it returns true if all input variables are true, otherwise false. Algebraic expression: $A \wedge B$
- OR: Denoted by the symbol ($\vee$), it returns true if at least one input variable is true, otherwise false. Algebraic expression: $A \vee B$.
- NOT: Denoted by the symbol ($\sim$), it negates the input variable, returning the opposite Boolean value. Algebraic expression: $\sim A$
- XOR: Denoted by the symbol $\oplus$, it returns true if an odd number of input variables are true, otherwise false. Algebraic expression: $A \oplus B$

The Boolean function is a mathematical function that takes n variables and returns a value in the set $\mathbb{B} = \{0, 1\}$. In other words, it operates on a set of binary inputs and produces a binary output. The number of variables, denoted as n, is a positive integer [8]. To represent all possible combinations of the n variables, we use the n-fold Cartesian product of the set $\mathbb{B}$ with itself, denoted as $\mathbb{B}^n$.

$$F : \{0,1\}^n \to \{0,1\}$$

Meaning $\{0,1\}^n$ set of all bit strings of length n, with 0 and 1 are bits. Let us suppose an algebric expression:

$$F_1 = X\overline{Y}Z$$

Then the value of F_1 will be 1, when $X = 1$, $\overline{Y} = 0$ and $C = 1$. For other values of X,$\overline{Y}$,Z the value of F_1 is 0.

Validity tables, logical formulas, or a combination of logical gates can be used to express Boolean functions. Truth tables include a list of all potential input-output pairs. Logical formulas explain the link between inputs and outputs using logical operators and variables. Logical gates are physical or electrical components used in digital circuits to implement Boolean functions. A truth table is a tabular representation of the outputs of a boolean function for all possible input variable combinations [9]. It gives a thorough picture of how the function behaves and helps in the analysis of its logic and advantages. For example, let us consider equation given as follow:

$$F_2 = Z + XY$$

The output will be 1 when $Z = 1$ and $XY = 1$ or when both of these are 1. For this equation, we get the total of the rows present in the truth table would be 2^n, where n number of variables (**Table 2**).

We aim to create hardware implementations of some very simple elementary gates (*OR*, *NOT*, and *AND*). By combining these operations, we can construct more complex circuits.

2.2 OR and AND: irreversible gates

Irreversible gates, such as the AND (∧) and OR(∨) gates, constitute crucial components of digital logic circuits. In contrast to reversible gates, irreversible gates cause information loss during operation and are frequently used within actual electronic circuits. In the case of a compound proposition of this type X ∧ Y must be true if both *X* and *Y* are true. In contrast, for X ∨ Y is true if either *X* or *Y* is true individually.

Z	X	Y	F_2
0	0	0	0
0	0	1	0
0	1	0	0
0	1	1	1
1	0	0	1
1	0	0	1
1	0	1	1
1	1	0	1
1	1	1	1

Table 2.
Boolean function table.

- **AND** gate output is going to equal 1 when both input bits are 1. It's circuit and truth table are (**Figure 1**).

- **OR** gate output is going to equal 1 if either of the input bits are 1. It's circuit and truth table are (**Figure 2**).

The OR gate, like the AND gate, is implemented in actual circuits using transistors and other electrical elements. Because the input states cannot be uniquely identified from the output, both the AND and OR gates are irreversible. In other words, if you know the result of an AND or OR gate, you cannot figure out what inputs produced that output. Reversible gates, on the other hand, allow for the complete recovery of input data from output data.

2.3 NAND and NOR: universal gates

In digital logic circuits, universal gates are ones that can be used to implement any other gate. The NAND gate and the NOR gate are two often used universal gates. NAND and NOR gates, as well as *AND*, *OR*, *NOT*, and *XOR* gates, can be used to build any other gate.

- **NAND** gate which stands for NOT of AND, and which outputs the NOT of the AND of the bits. It's circuit and truth table are (**Figure 3**).

- **NOR** gate, which stands for NOT of OR, and which outputs the NOT of the OR of the bits. It's circuit and truth table are (**Figure 4**).

The NAND gate is created by combining an AND gate and a NOT gate. It takes two binary inputs, X and Y, and outputs the logical inverse of the AND operation. If both inputs are 1, the output is 0; else the output is 1. The NOR gate accepts two binary inputs, A and B, and outputs the logical inverse of the OR operator. Only if both inputs are 0 is the output 1; if not the output is 0. Because of their versatility and

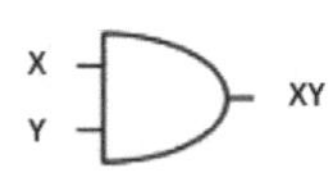

X	Y	X ∧ Y
0	0	0
0	1	0
1	0	0
1	1	1

Figure 1.
Circuit diagram for the AND logical irreversible gate and the truth table.

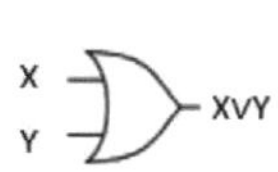

X	Y	X ∨ Y
0	0	0
0	1	1
1	0	1
1	1	1

Figure 2.
Circuit diagram for the OR logical irreversible gate and the truth table.

ability to implement any other gate, NAND and NOR gates are frequently employed in digital logic circuits and computer architectures.

2.4 SWAP, NOT and CNOT: reversible gates

An even more complicated gate is SWAP gate, it is an exchange of bits (2 inputs, 2 outputs), it a common gate between classical and quantum computer, To generate the effect of a SWAP operation, some action has to take place. A SWAP gate icon that is more common in quantum circuit designs. The reason for having a different icon for SWAP in quantum circuits than in classical circuits is because many quantum circuit implementations do not have physical wires. As consequence, representing a SWAP operation as a wire crossing may be misleading. Instead, a SWAP operation can be accomplished using a number of applied fields (**Figure 5**).

The NOT gate is often employed in classical computing for many kinds of functions such as logical operations, binary arithmetic, and controlling data flow in digital circuits. It is one of the fundamental components that are used in the making of more complicated logic circuits and computer systems. In computer programming, the NOT gate is also used to complement binary integers and execute bitwise NOT operations. The NOT Gate is a single reversible gate, it takes a single input bit and get a single output bit. If the input bit is 0, the NOT gate outputs 1, else it outputs 0 (**Figure 6**).

The Controlled-NOT (CNOT) gate is not a normal gate in classical computing like the AND, OR, or NOT gates, but its functionality can be resembled using other classical logic gates. The CNOT gate is a two-qubit gate that performs a controlled

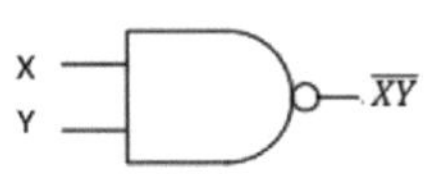

X	Y	$\overline{XY}$
0	0	1
0	1	1
1	0	1
1	1	0

Figure 3.
Circuit diagram for the NAND logical universal gate and the truth table.

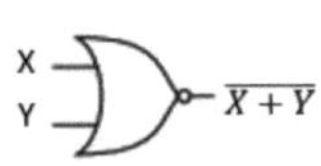

X	Y	$\overline{X+Y}$
0	0	1
0	1	0
1	0	0
1	1	0

Figure 4.
Circuit diagram for the NOR logical universal gate and the truth table.

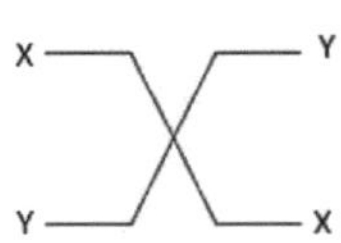

X	Y	X'	Y'
0	0	0	0
0	1	1	0
1	0	0	1
1	1	1	1

Figure 5.
Circuit diagram for the SWAP gate and the truth table.

DOI: http://dx.doi.org/10.5772/intechopen.1002792

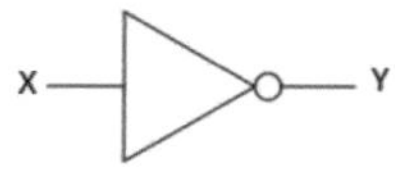

X	Y
0	1
1	0

Figure 6.
Circuit diagram for the NOT gate and the truth table.

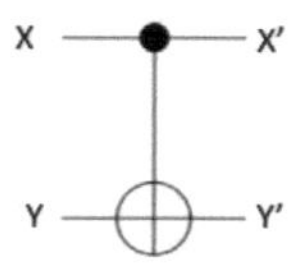

X	Y	X'	Y'
0	0	0	0
0	1	0	1
1	0	1	1
1	1	1	0

Figure 7.
Circuit diagram for the CNOT gate and the truth table.

NOT operation on the second qubit dependent on the state of the first qubit in quantum computing. A combination of AND, OR, and NOT gates can be used to achieve the functionality (**Figure 7**).

Although the classical CNOT gate, which is implemented using AND, OR and NOT gates can achieve functionality, as the CNOT gate it's important to note that the classical implementation lacks reversibility. Reversible computing pertains to a concept where all operations and gates are designed in such a way that information can be accurately retrieved from the output. Unfortunately this classical CNOT implementation does not fulfill that requirement.

2.5 Is all Boolean circuits can be simulated reversibly?

On the side reversible computing is a type of computing approach that focuses on carrying out computations in a manner that preserves information. This means that the original inputs can be retrieved uniquely from the outputs. Reversible computing is closely tied to the concept of information conservation. Requires that the number of inputs, to a circuit matches the number of outputs. However traditional Boolean circuits used in classical computing suffer from information loss due to operations such as AND and OR gates [10]. These gates lead to information loss making it impossible to recover the inputs with certainty, from the outputs. Reversible computing is closely connected to information conservation, and the number of inputs to a reversible circuit must be the same as the number of outputs. Many Classical Boolean circuits used in classical computing, on the other hand, contain fundamental information loss due to irreversible operations such as AND and OR gates. These gates generate information loss, make it impossible to figure out the original inputs from the outputs in an unusual way. Consider a simple AND gate with two inputs A and B and a single output C. The output C is 1, if both X and Y are 1, and 0 for all other input combinations. If we know W is 0, we cannot tell if X and Y were both 0 or one of them was 1 [11]. As a result of this, because information about the original inputs is lost, this AND gate is irreversible. Certain gates, such as the Controlled-NOT (CNOT) gate in quantum computing, are reversible and can be simulated reversibly. In quantum computing, the CNOT gate is usually used to implement reversible logic operations.

- Reversible simulation is impossible: If a Boolean circuit F is irreversible, at least one input combination (X_i) gives the same output (W_j) as another input combination (X_k) giving the same output (W_j). If $X_i \neq X_k$ exists such that $F(X_i) = F(X_k)$ for some output index j (W_j), then F is irreversible.

- Let us prove it by contradiction: Let us assume a reversible simulation of the irreversible circuit F exists. This reversible simulation would have created different results for all possible input combinations. However, because F is irreversible, there are input combinations X_i and X_k $(X_i \neq$ of $X_k)$ in which $F(X_i) = F(X_k)$. The reversible simulation cannot find X_i and X_k uniquely from the same output, which put us in a contradiction.

The bit is the smallest unit of classical information, with two possible states: 0 or 1. Information can be encoded using bits. Logic gates such as NOT, AND, OR, XOR, NAND, and NOR operate on bits. These gates, when we put them together, we are allowed do any computation, and combination of these gates, such as NOT, AND, OR, and NAND, that are also universal. Classical computers can handle some problems and calculations quickly, but others take a long time to find the solution, and it might be correct or faults. Some tasks that are difficult for classical computers, that's why they are thought to be solved by quantum computers.

3. Quantum computing

After examining both irreversible and reversible gates we gained a deeper understanding of the advantages offered by quantum gates. In the domain of computation a series of logic gates operates on a limited number of classical bits at once. Similarly in quantum computation a sequence of quantum logic gates acts on a qubits at a time to represent the process. The primary difference is that classical logic gates manipulate classical bit values, either 0 or 1, yet quantum gates can manipulate complicated multi-partite quantum states, including arbitrary superpositions of computational base states, which are frequently entangled [12]. As a consequence, the logic circuits used in quantum computation have a much wider range of operations than those used in classical computation. At the present, certain industries are building quantum computers on a limited scale. The development of quantum computers confronts obstacles as the number of factors that influence their performance and limit their scale. To properly illustrate quantum characteristics, qubits must be maintained in a controlled environment where all qubits function in a correlated manner. Even tiny changes in the quantum system's environment may perturb the qubits and even initiate a system crash. By following the laws of quantum physics, quantum computers present several states at once, and establish a vessel of correlation between them, which extremely enhances its processing powers [13].

3.1 Quantum dynamics

The Schrödinger equation is at the foundation of quantum dynamics, describing how the quantum state of a system grows over time [14]. It's the basis of quantum mechanics and provides insights into the behavior of particles and wavefunctions. The time-dependent Schrödinger equation is given by

$$i\hbar\frac{\partial}{\partial t}|\Psi(t)\rangle = H|\Psi(t)\rangle \tag{1}$$

where i represents the imaginary unit, $\hbar$ denotes the reduced Planck constant, $\frac{\partial}{\partial t}|\Psi(t)\rangle$ signifies the partial derivative of the quantum state $|\Psi(t)\rangle$ with respect to t, and H stands for the Hamiltonian operator, which encapsulates the total energy of the quantum system. In numerous instances, the Hamiltonian operator can be expressed as the combination of the kinetic energy (T) and potential energy (V) operators, i.e., $H = T + V$. The kinetic energy operator T is derived from the momentum operator p squared, divided by twice the mass m, thus yielding $T = p^2/2m$. Conversely, the potential energy operator V hinges on the spatial coordinates of the system and represents the interaction energies within the system.

The time-dependent Schrödinger equation provides a mathematical framework to predict the future behavior of a quantum system, given its initial state and the Hamiltonian operator. Solving this equation allows us to determine how the quantum state $|\Psi(t)\rangle$ evolves over time. It's important to note that the Schrödinger equation is a cornerstone of non-relativistic quantum mechanics. For relativistic particles, such as those moving at velocity close to the speed of light, a more comprehensive equation known as the Dirac equation is used. Solving the Schrödinger equation for complex quantum systems, especially those involving multiple particles, can be challenging. Numerical methods, approximations, and simplifications are often employed for getting insights into the behavior of quantum systems [15]. The Schrödinger equation captures the concept of quantum dynamics by characterizing the time evolution of quantum states in response to the Hamiltonian operator. It's an effective equation that supports much of our understanding of quantum mechanics and plays a crucial role in fields that extend from atomic and molecular physics to quantum computing. The Schrödinger equation expand on its significance and dig into its mathematical form in more details, like the "wave function evolution" of a quantum system over time, while the wavefunction contains all the information about the quantum state, including the probabilities of various measurement outcomes, by solving the Schrödinger equation allows us to know how these probabilities vary in time. We have also the Superposition described by the Schrödinger equation, any system in quantum mechanics can exist in superposition, unless we disturb this superposition influencing the probabilities of various outcomes, and the Schrödinger equation explains how these superpositions evolve.

3.2 Quantum superposition

In the complicated field of quantum mechanics, a phenomenon known as superposition comes up as a remarkable characteristic that defies classical intuition. Superposition entails the difficult ability of quantum systems to exist in a variety of states simultaneously, confusing the conventional binary distinction. The Schrödinger equation, which we previously examined in greater detail, plays a pivotal role in describing the dynamics of superposition and offers a mathematical framework for comprehending the coexistence of multiple states within a single quantum entity [16]. This extraordinary trait introduces a profound shift in how we comprehend the fundamental constituents of the universe, driving us beyond classical boundaries into a domain where particles and systems can effectively traverse a multiplicity of potential states. As we begin on an exploration to learn about the complex nature of superposition, we will delve into its implications, manifestations, and the intriguing ways it intersects with the Schrödinger equation. Through this investigation, we will uncover the remarkable aspects of superposition that reveal the fascinating nature of quantum reality. As we explained previously the qubit is in a superposition, meaning that it can be in state $|0\rangle$ and $|1\rangle$ at the same time, we described by the follow equation:

$$|\Psi\rangle = \frac{1}{\sqrt{2}}(|0\rangle + |1\rangle)$$

This exciting concept is beautifully captured by the Bloch vector, a pointer extending from the sphere's center, which traces out the qubit's trip through superposition [17]. The Bloch sphere offers an actual means to intuitively comprehend the complicity of probabilities that define superposition, providing both a theoretical framework and a geometrical sphere for investigating the remarkable nature of quantum states (**Figure 8**).

We can also demonstrate states with an imaginary and complex numbers that are used in quantum computing. In quantum mechanics, complex numbers provide an essential role in representing quantum states and transformations. When representing quantum states on the Bloch sphere, the horizontal angle corresponds to the phase of complex probability amplitudes. This phase, encoded in the complex numbers, contributes to interference phenomena and the observed probabilities of measurement outcomes. Moreover, the Bloch sphere's vertical angle represents the probability amplitudes themselves, blending real and imaginary components to define the state's position. Complex numbers introduce an additional dimension to the Bloch sphere, allowing us to obtain the full meaning of quantum superposition and entanglement. By adopting the mathematics of imaginary and complex numbers, the Bloch sphere in which we can determine the quantum states and provide behaviors of the quantum state (**Figure 9**).

In the domain of quantum physics, the Bloch sphere serves as a bridge between the abstract and the visual, giving a unique view into the quantum states behavior. Through its elegant representation, we open a better knowledge of superposition, entanglement, and the probabilities that include the quantum field. As we move the surface of the Bloch sphere, led by the mathematics of imaginary and complex numbers, we discover a dimension where particles may occupy several states

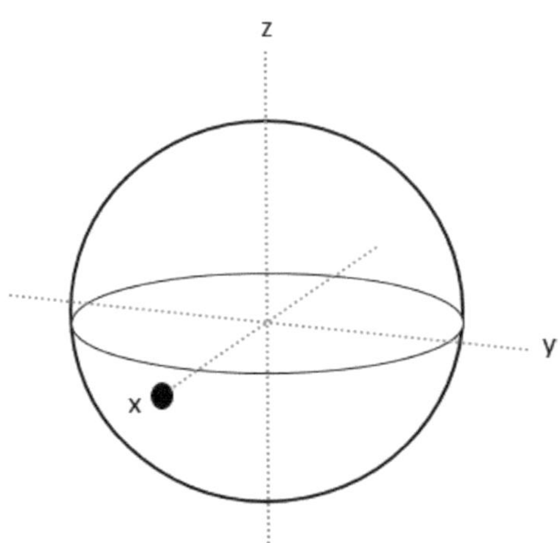

Figure 8.
Bloch sphere where the state is at the (x, y, z) point $(1,0,0)$, where the Bloch sphere intersects the x axis.

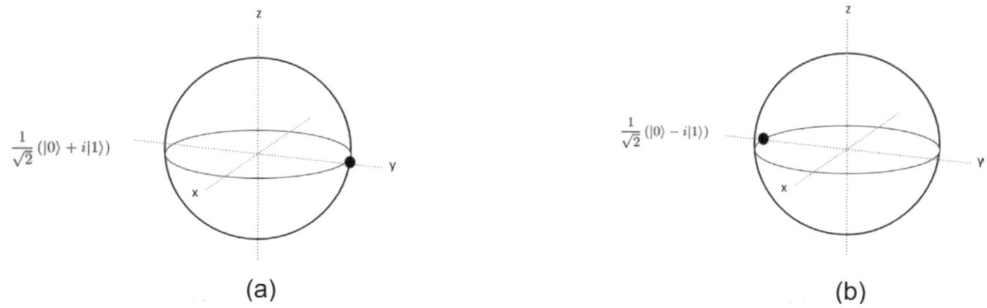

Figure 9.
Bloch sphere where in (a) the state is at the y axis at point (0,1,0)*, in (b) the state is at the y axis at point* (0, −1, 0)*.*

simultaneously. This understanding helps us understand the significance of quantum sates. The Bloch sphere helps us see beyond the limitations of classical understanding.

3.3 Quantum entanglement

Entanglement, a phenomenon at the basis of quantum mechanics, is both mysterious and fascinating. It defines a unique state where the properties of two or more particles become correlated in such a way that their individual quantum states cannot be described independently [17]. Instead, they are intricately linked, regardless of the distance between them. This remarkable connection challenges our classical intuitions and has profound implications for our understanding of the nature of reality. Imagine two entangled particles, often referred to as "spooky action at a distance" by Einstein, Podolsky, and Rosen (EPR) in their famous thought experiment. When the quantum state of one particle is measured, the state of the other particle instantly "collapses" into a corresponding state, no matter how far apart they are. This instantaneous correlation defies our classical notions of causality and presents concerns about the true nature of information transfer in the quantum field. Entanglement is beautifully visualized in the context of the Bloch sphere. Imagine two entangled particles, each represented by a Bloch vector on its own sphere. These vectors are intrinsically linked such that if you measure the spin of one particle along a certain axis, the other particle's spin will be immediately known along the same axis, regardless of the distance separating them. This phenomenon has significant practical implications, particularly in the emerging field of quantum computing and quantum communication. Entanglement functions as a resource to perform operations that are not classically possible, enabling quantum computers to potentially solve intricate problems at an exponential speedup compared to classical computers. Furthermore, entanglement-based quantum communication has the promise of secure communication protocols, where any spying would disrupt the delicate entanglement and thus be detectable [18]. Yet, entanglement also raises significant philosophical concerns about the nature of reality and how we fit in the universe. It challenges the notion of local reality, suggesting that our world may not operate according to the intuitive classical principles we have come to expect.

Let us proceed to the subject of entanglement using mathematics to get a more complete understand. Entanglement happens when two or more quantum systems become paired in such a way that their individual states cannot be represented separately [19]. Mathematically, let us imagine a system of two qubits, A and B. Their combined state, represented as a tensor product, can be stated as:

$$|\Psi_{AB}\rangle = \alpha|0_A\rangle \otimes \beta|1_B\rangle - \beta|1_A\rangle \otimes \alpha|0_B\rangle \tag{2}$$

Here, α and β are complex probability amplitudes, $|0_A\rangle$ and $|1_B\rangle$ represent the basis states of qubit A, and $|0_B\rangle$ and $|1_B\rangle$ represent the basis states of qubit B.

Bell states are unique entangled states with the strongest correlation. One such Bell state is the singlet state:

$$|\Psi^-\rangle = \frac{1}{\sqrt{2}}(|0_A\rangle \otimes |1_B\rangle - |1_A\rangle \otimes |0_B\rangle) \tag{3}$$

When measuring the first qubit in the singlet state along the Z axis (spin measurement), the second qubit's state quickly collapses to the opposite consequence. If qubit A is measured as $|0\rangle$, qubit B will be $|1\rangle$, and vice versa. Mathematically, this could be written as: If A is measured as $|0_A\rangle$, then B is $|1_B\rangle$, and vice versa.

In the context of entanglement, the Einstein-Podolsky-Rosen (EPR) problem reveals the non-local character of quantum correlations. The EPR argument includes two entangled particles, A and B, in a singlet state $|\Psi^-\rangle$. The spin measurements in a specified direction for each particle are characterized by operators S_{Az} ad S_{Bz}, where S_{Ax} denotes the spin operator for particle A along the x-axis. These operators have eigenvalues of $\pm\frac{\hbar}{2}$, signifying the two probable results of measurement. The EPR argument focuses on the correlation between the measurements of particles A and B along the same axis. By measuring the spin of particle A along the x axis S_{Ax} and particle B along the x axis S_{Bx} gives us:

$$S_{Ax}|\Psi^-\rangle = \frac{\hbar}{2}|\Psi^-\rangle, \qquad S_{Bx}|\Psi^-\rangle = -\frac{\hbar}{2}|\Psi^-\rangle. \tag{4}$$

It means that if particle A is found with spin up in the x-direction, particle B will be found with spin down, and vice versa. This quick correlation across space, no matter the distance between the particles, is a key component of the EPR paradox and what Einstein referred to as "spooky action at a distance". Bell's inequality is an equation that quantifies the correlations predicted between measurements on entangled particles offered they meet local reality, a classical idea that argues that physical attributes are predetermined and do not change instantly. For a system including the measurement angles θ and ϕ for particles A and B, Bell's inequality is generally written as: $S(\theta,\phi)\leqslant 2$, here, $S(\theta,\phi)$ is the correlation function that measures the correlation between the measurement outputs. If the measured correlation exceeds the value of 2, it indicates a violation of Bell's inequality and suggests that the observed correlations cannot be explained by local realism. Experimental studies of Bell's inequality have demonstrated violations, showing the non-local and non classical nature of entanglement. Violations of Bell's inequality suggest that the entangled particles are connected in ways that cannot be explained by traditional physics (**Figure 10**) [20].

$$H = \frac{1}{\sqrt{2}}\begin{pmatrix} 1 & 1 \\ 1 & -1 \end{pmatrix}$$

3.4 Pauli spin matrices

Pauli spin matrices are the mathematical tools in quantum physics that represent the fundamental momentum, or spin of particles, especially fermions like electrons.

$$H = \frac{1}{\sqrt{2}}\begin{pmatrix} 1 & 1 \\ 1 & -1 \end{pmatrix}$$

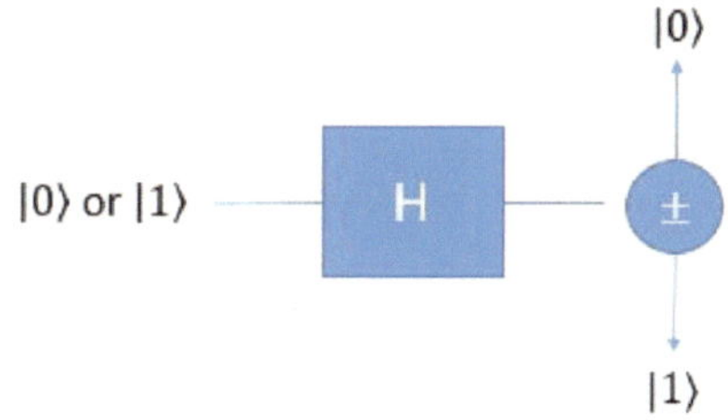

Figure 10.
Hadamard gate.

Expressed as matrices, these operators give an approach for expressing the spin states and interactions of particles [21]. The Pauli spin matrices, indicated by σ_x, σ_y and σ_z, are fundamental for understanding different quantum system. They are defined as follows in their matrix form:

$$\sigma_x = \begin{pmatrix} 0 & 1 \\ 1 & 0 \end{pmatrix}, \quad \sigma_y = \begin{pmatrix} 0 & -i \\ i & 0 \end{pmatrix}, \quad \sigma_z = \begin{pmatrix} 1 & 0 \\ 0 & -1 \end{pmatrix} \tag{5}$$

These matrices describe spin observables along three orthogonal axes in a quantum system. When applied to spin $-1/2$ particles, like electrons, the Pauli spin matrices generate a set of eigenstates combining to the possible spin measurements in each direction. The commutation relations between these matrices show the non-commutative character of spin observables, which is a hallmark of quantum mechanics. The Pauli matrices find use in many different applications, from expressing spin states of particles to creating quantum gates in quantum computing. Their elegant matrix representations include the complex behavior of quantum spins, contributing significantly to the development and understanding of quantum mechanics [22].

Quantum gates are important in building blocks of quantum computing, letting the control and transformation of qubits, the basic units of quantum information. These gates are represented as unitary matrices which operate on the quantum state vector. Quantum gates perform a function similar to traditional logic gates, but with the extra complexity of superposition and entanglement. One of the most fundamental quantum gates is the Hadamard gate (H), which creates superpositions between qubits, it is described by the matrix: We apply the Hadamard gate to qubits as follow:

$$H|0\rangle = \frac{1}{\sqrt{2}}(|0\rangle + |1\rangle), \quad H|1\rangle = \frac{1}{\sqrt{2}}(|0\rangle - |1\rangle). \tag{6}$$

Another significant gate is the Pauli-X gate, σ_x, which performs a bit-flip operation, and the phase change is done by the Pauli-Y gate σ_y and the Pauli-Z σ_z gate. Quantum gates can be coupled to create complicated quantum circuits. For instance, the Controlled-NOT (CNOT) gate, a two qubit gate, flips the target qubit if and only if the control qubit is $|1\rangle$, and it is represented by the matrix: The application of quantum gates lets us create quantum algorithms and perform operations using the concepts of superposition and entanglement. These gates constitute the basis of quantum computing and provide the possibility for addressing difficult problems beyond the capability of classical computers. The Pauli-X gate (X or σ_x) is a fundamental quantum gate that functions as a bit-flip operation, similar to the conventional NOT gate.

$$CNOT = \begin{pmatrix} 1 & 0 & 0 & 0 \\ 0 & 1 & 0 & 0 \\ 0 & 0 & 0 & 1 \\ 0 & 0 & 1 & 0 \end{pmatrix}$$

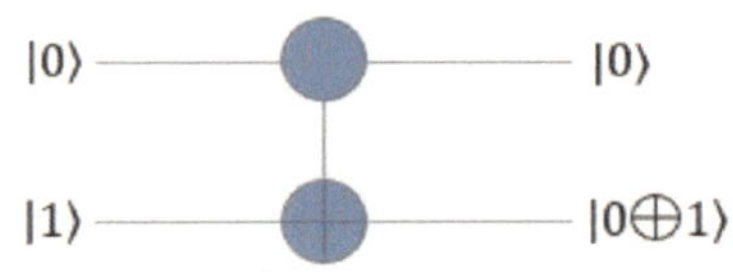

Figure 11.
The CNOT gate.

$$X = \sigma_x = \begin{pmatrix} 0 & 1 \\ 1 & 0 \end{pmatrix}$$

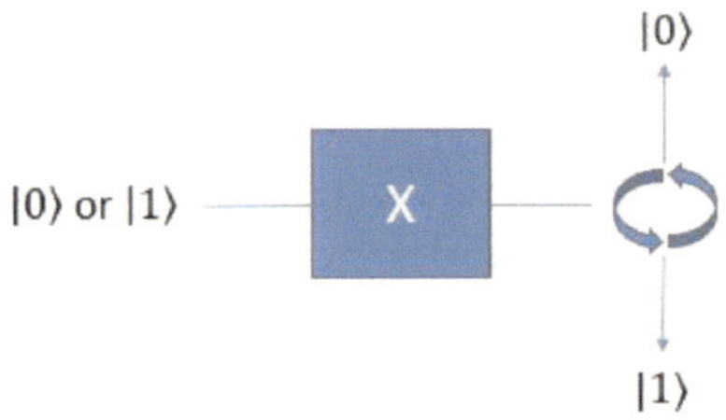

Figure 12.
the NOT gate.

Mathematically, the Pauli-X gate is represented by the matrix: we apply the X gate to the qubits as follow (**Figures 11** and **12**).

$$X|0\rangle = |1\rangle) \qquad X|1\rangle = |0\rangle \tag{7}$$

In the Bloch sphere represented, the Pauli-X gate flips the quantum state vector across the x-axis. This gate is important because it puts the basis for quantum error correction, quantum cryptography, and is an essential component in several quantum algorithms [23]. By combining the Pauli-X gate with other quantum gates like the Hadamard gate, Pauli-Y gate, and Pauli-Z gate, we can create quantum circuits that execute complex operations on qubits. These gates, functioning in the domain of superposition and entanglement, allow quantum computers to deal with problems that are impossible for classical computers, offering a new generation of computing and scientific growth [24].

4. Quantum data compression

To begin, we'll need a number that indicates how much knowledge you'd acquire if you knew the quantum state of some system. The Von Neumann entropy is an appropriate quantity [25]:

$$S(\rho) = -Tr\rho \log \rho, \tag{8}$$

where the trace operation and ρ is the density operator characterizing a quantum system's ensemble of states. This is in contrast to the traditional Shannon entropy.

$$S(\{p(x)\}) = -\sum_x p(x) \log_2 p(x). \tag{9}$$

Assume that the probability distribution of a classical random variable X is $p(x)$. The density matrix of a quantum system prepared in a state $|x\rangle$ dictated by the value of X is $\sum_x p(x)|x\rangle\langle x|$, where the states $|x\rangle$ need not be orthogonal. $S(\rho)$ is demonstrated to represent an upper limit on the classical mutual information $I(X:Y)$ between X and the outcome Y of a system measurement. We analyze the resources required to store or communicate the state of a quantum system q' of density matrix ρ to create a link using qubits. The goal is to gather $n \gg 1$ of these systems and transmit the combined state into a smaller system. The smaller system is broadcast down the channel, and the combined state is decoded at the receiving end into n systems q of the same kind as q. Each q's final density matrix is ρ', and the entire process is considered successful if ρ is sufficiently close to the desired state. The fidelity defined by is a measure of resemblance between two density matrices [26].

$$f(\rho,\rho') = \left(\left(Tr\sqrt{\rho^{1/2}\rho'\rho^{1/2}}\right)\right)^2. \tag{10}$$

This can be read as the likelihood that q will pass a test to determine if it is in the state ρ. The fidelity is none other than the classic overlap: $f = \| |\varphi\rangle\langle\varphi| \|^2$ when ρ and ρ' are both pure states, $|\varphi\rangle\langle\varphi|$ and $|\varphi'\rangle\langle\varphi'|$. The complete state of n systems is represented by a vector in a Hilbert space of 2^n dimensions, if we limit ourselves to $2state$ systems for simplicity. If the Von Neumann entropy $S(\rho)\langle 1$, the state vector is very likely to lie in a typical Hilbert space subspace in any given realization.

Moreover, the encoding and decoding operations are blind: they do not require knowledge of the precise states that are being communicated. The *encoding* and *decoding* necessary to produce such quantum data compression and decompression are technically challenging. It is currently impossible to do so using photons. It is, nevertheless, the maximum compression permitted by the rules of physics.
Other classical notions like Huffman coding, as well as the fundamental concept of information, have quantum equivalents [27]. In addition, Schumacher and Nielson develop a number called "coherent information," which is a measure of mutual information for quantum systems. It encompasses the portion of mutual information between entangled systems that cannot be accounted for using traditional methods. This is an excellent method to comprehend the Bell–EPR relationships.

5. Quantum information protocols

5.1 Quantum key distribution

Quantum cryptography is a branch of research that uses quantum mechanics principles to encrypt and transmit data so that hackers cannot access it. The development and execution of various cryptographic tasks using the unique capabilities and power of quantum computers are also included in the larger use of quantum cryptography. Quantum computers have the potential to help the creation of new, stronger, and more efficient encryption methods that would be difficult to create using current computing and communication infrastructures [28]. The following are two popular, although quite different cryptography applications that are being developed using quantum properties:

- Quantum key distribution: is the act of having a common key between two trusted parties utilizing quantum communication so that an untrusted "eavesdropper" cannot learn anything about the key.

- Quantum safe cryptography: is the development of cryptographic algorithms, also defined as post-quantum cryptography, that are secure against a quantum computer attack and may be used to provide quantum-safe certificates.

Quantum Key Distribution (QKD) entails transmitting encrypted data via networks as classical bits, while the keys to decode the data are encoded and sent as qubits in a quantum state. For implementing QKD, many methods, or protocols, have been devised. This is how BB84, a frequently used one, operates. Imagine Alice and Bob, two humans. Alice wants to transmit Bob info in a secure manner. To accomplish so, she builds a qubit based encryption key whose polarization states reflect the key's individual bit values.

"Decoherence" will force some of the qubits' delicate quantum states to collapse as they travel to their destination. To account for this, Alice and Bob do "key distillation," which entails determining if the error rate is high enough to indicate that a hacker has attempted to intercept the key. If that's the case, they discard the suspicious key and continue to generate new ones until they are certain they are sharing a secure one. Alice may then use hers to encrypt data and send it to Bob in classical bits, which he can decode using his key [29].

5.2 The BB84 protocol for distributing quantum keys

Charles Bennett and Gilles Brassard devised the first quantum key distribution technique in 1984, which is also known as BB84 [30]. The system is based on the dispersion of single photons or particles. The polarization of a photon will encode the value of a classical bit. We'd want to convey some facts about photons and the quantum mechanical description utilized in the protocol before we describe the BB84 system.

With quantum cryptography, the key is a stream of photons, photons have a property called spin that can be changed as soon as it pass by filter. We have two groups of filers rectilinear $|\uparrow\rangle$, $|\rightarrow\rangle$ and diagonal $|\nwarrow\rangle$, $|\nearrow\rangle$. The state of $|\rightarrow\rangle$ and $|\nearrow\rangle$ codes 1 while $|\uparrow\rangle$ and $|\nwarrow\rangle$ codes 0. Alice decides whether to encode her random number using a rectilinear or diagonal basis at random for each transmission. Each photon's polarization is now picked at random from a set of ($|\uparrow\rangle$, $|\rightarrow\rangle$, $|\nwarrow\rangle$, $|\nearrow\rangle$), making it impossible for Eve to identify its polarization state. Because a $|\nwarrow\rangle$ or $|\nearrow\rangle$ polarized photon has the same chance of being projected into either horizontal or vertical polarization state (we call it a measurement in rectilinear basis), Eve will destroy information encoded in diagonal basis if she uses a polarization beam splitter to project the input photon into either horizontal or vertical polarization state (we call it a measurement in rectilinear basis). Eve and Bob are perplexed since none of them knows which basis Alice will pick ahead of time. Bob picks either a rectilinear or a diagonal basis to measure each incoming photon at random, unaware of Alice's basis decision. Alice and Bob can create correlated random bits if they both utilize the same basis [31]. Their bit values, on the other hand, are uncorrelated if they employ distinct bases. After Bob has measured all of the photons, he uses an authorized public channel to compare his measurement bases with Alice. They only maintain sifting keys, which are random bits produced with matching bases. Their filtered keys are identical and may be utilized as a secure key without ambient sounds, system flaws, or Eve's interference.

- Alice picks the basis and polarization of her photons at random and transmits them to Bob. She wishes to send a string of bits 110,101,101,001, for example. She will pick a basis (either horizontal or vertical) at random for each bit, as illustrated in 1.13.

- Bob picks a basis at random for each photon he receives and uses it to measure that photon. If he uses the same basis as Alice, he will get the same result, i.e. the interpreted bit will be accurate. If he picks a different foundation, though, he will get either 0 or 1 with equal likelihood. As a result, this is a completely random process in which some bits will be correctly translated while others will be incorrect. 1.13 depicts Bob's measuring procedure and the bases he picked at random. A raw key is a series of interpreted bits like Bob's. As a result, Alice's raw key is the first set of bits she sent to Bob.

- Bob utilizes the public channel to communicate with Alice in order to figure out which parts he got right. He does not provide the measurement's findings, i.e. the raw key, but rather the foundation on which each Alice's photon was received. If Alice uses the same foundation for each photon, she will have an agreement with Bob. If Alice's foundation differs from Bob's, she declares a dispute. This may be seen in the image above. Both Alice and Bob then filter their raw keys to get a shorter sequence of bits called a sifted key by removing bits associated with unpleasant bases (**Figure 13**).

As a result, if Alice and Bob utilized the same basis for a photon, whether rectilinear or diagonal, they should have the same filtered keys. The filtered key, according to theory, will be the secret key. However, this is only true when dealing with a flawless experiment. In the actual world, the environment will alter the polarization of photons in optical fiber, or Eve will corrupt certain photons during eavesdropping owing to an incorrectly selected foundation. As a result, the filtered keys of Alice and Bob will not match, indicating that Eve is listening in. Alice and Bob pose the filtered keys, which are not equal in practice, after the three major phases of the BB84 protocol. In that

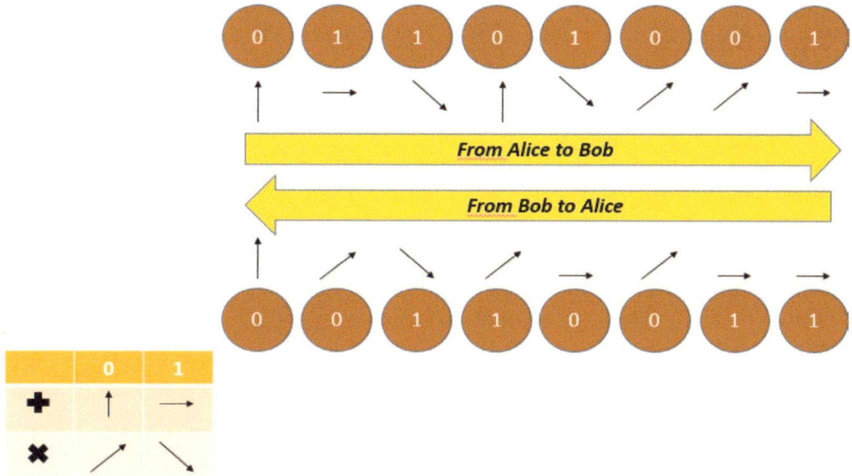

Figure 13.
Alice delivers the photons, which are all programmed on a random basis.

case, a few more steps are required: estimation of the transmission error rate based on a random sample from both sides' raw keys (random bits are then discarded from the raw keys); extraction of the reconciled key, i.e. error free common key, using some error correction methods; and, finally, privacy amplification, i.e. extraction of the reconciled key.

Other QKD methods follow the same stages as the ones we have listed here. EPR and B92 QKD methods are also available for information purposes only. The B92 protocol may be simplified to BB84, but the EPR procedure employs quantum-correlated particles, which are photon pairs created by certain particle processes. Various QKD protocols are given, as well as explanations of particular error correcting methods.

As we go further into the domain of quantum mechanics, we switch our focusing from the basic concepts of quantum gates and entanglement to study two events that demonstrate the unique character of the quantum universe. The first of these is the idea of non-cloning, a concept that contradicts standard concepts of replicating information. In the quantum domain, perfect copying of arbitrary quantum states is disallowed owing to the famous "no-cloning theorem," which we shall unravel via its mathematical expression. Building upon this, we will next go into the interesting notion of quantum teleportation, a method that permits the transmission of quantum information from one point to another without physical movement. Through mathematical equations, we will explore the complicated mechanics behind these events and reveal the potential they provide in the field of quantum information [32].

5.3 No-cloning

There is no unitary operator that can clone arbitrary qubit, unless the state has previously been determined. The unitary operator can be express as a circuit (**Figure 14**).

Where $|\omega\rangle = |0\rangle$, mathematically we can say $U(|\Psi\rangle|\omega\rangle) = |\Psi\rangle|\Psi\rangle$. Let us proof that cloning is not linear and hence cannot be unitary, We think about the situation $|\Psi\rangle = |\alpha\rangle + |\beta\rangle$, we have $U(|\Psi\rangle|0\rangle) = |\alpha\alpha\rangle + |\beta\beta\rangle \neq |\Psi\rangle|\Psi\rangle$. Each particular cloning operation U can work on certain states (in the case above $|\alpha\rangle$ and $|\beta\rangle$), but because U is trace preserving, two clonable states must be orthogonal, $\langle\alpha|\beta\rangle = 0$. When special relativity principles are addressed, EPR correlations might be used to communicate faster than light if cloning were possible. This would result in a contradiction; an effect before a cause [33].

5.4 Super dense coding

Classical information can be stored and transmitted using qubits. Super dense coding significantly improves quantum communication by allowing two bits of

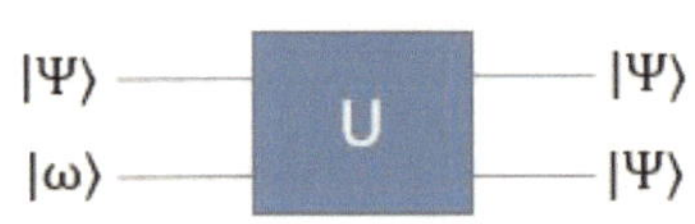

Figure 14.
Unitary operator circuit.

information to be sent using only one qubit [34]. This is achieved through the creation, manipulation, and measurement of entangled states [35].

$$0 = 00$$
$$1 = 01$$
$$2 = 10$$
$$3 = 11$$

It take two ordinary bits; each probably consisting of servel thousand atoms)to express the same amount of informations. Alice $'A'$ can send Bob $'B'$ first prepare an entangled Bell state and each takes one qubit from that state, thus setting us their communication apparatus (**Figure 15**).

When Alice is ready, she authors one of the four two bits messages, she then runs her entangled qubit; which is her half of Bell state; through a unitary logic gate $\{I, X, Y, Z\}$ which is determined by the message she wants to send. Alice ships her qubits off to Bob, who'll have the complete *entangled* bipartite state $|\beta_{00}\rangle$ (the full entangled pair), with:

$$|\beta_{00}\rangle = \frac{|00\rangle + |11\rangle}{\sqrt{2}}, \quad |\beta_{01}\rangle = \frac{|01\rangle + |10\rangle}{\sqrt{2}}, \quad |\beta_{10}\rangle = \frac{|00\rangle - |11\rangle}{\sqrt{2}}, \quad |\beta_{10}\rangle = \frac{|01\rangle - |10\rangle}{\sqrt{2}} \tag{11}$$

Bob measures his bipartite state along the Bell basis. Which Bell gate is a combination of *CNOT* and the first order *Hadamard*. Bob will get one of the four values. The resulting measurement will reveal the message. We can create a circuit for the superdense coding method as a whole:

- the transmission of traditional bits.
- Classical bits based on decisions.
- Communication between communicators is noiseless (**Figure 16**).

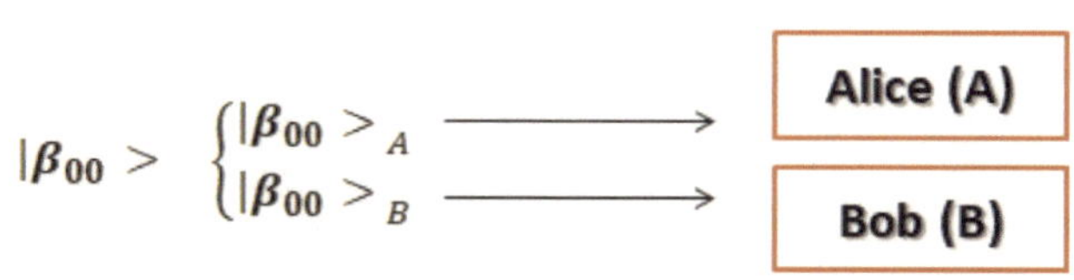

Figure 15.
The two halves of the entangled bell state's creation and distribution.

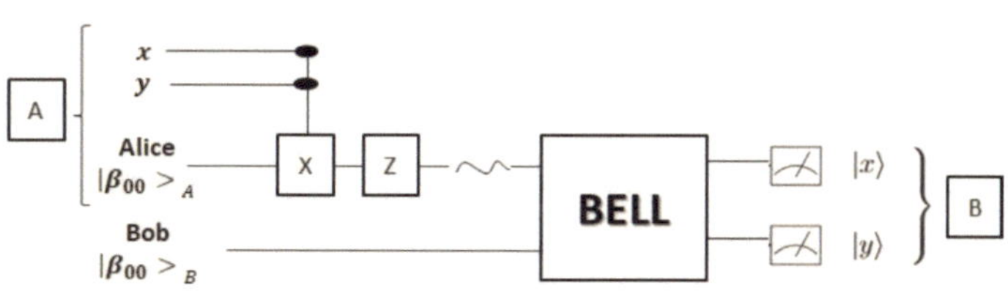

Figure 16.
The superdense coding circuit.

Alice controls (filled circles) which of the four operations (1, X, Z, or iY) she will perform to her qubit using her two-bit classical message xy. Bob measures both qubits along the Bell basis after transmitting her qubit to bob to retrieve the message xy, which is now sitting in the output registers in natural z-basis form $|x\rangle, |y\rangle$.

5.5 Quantum teleportation

At the heart of quantum teleportation are two important principles: entanglement and quantum superposition. Quantum superposition, on the other hand, allows particles to exist in numerous states simultaneously, until a measurement collapses the superposition into a definitive state [36]. Quantum Teleportation is when Alice transmitted Bob one qubit, $|\psi\rangle = \ |0\rangle + |1\rangle$, in superdense coding to reassemble two classical bits. The mirror counterpart of this technique is quantum teleportation. Alice wishes to communicate Bob the qubit, $|\psi\rangle$, using only two traditional bits of information. Alice's goal is to send to Bob a complete qubit, which contains a value that represents one of the infinitely possible superposition that can a state be in. The two prepare their communication channel by preparing their *Bell* state, and each one is taking one components qubits. Next, Alice produces the general state $|\psi_c\rangle$ for teleportation, but she has to get to Bob without sending the $|\psi_c\rangle$, instead she feeds ket-psi along with her half of the Bell state into a binary gate, so Alice measure the output of that gate, she end up with one of four classical strings (00,01,10,11) [37, 38]. Alice sends her two classical bits to Bob; who uses them to decide how to process his half of entanglement Bell pair, after he does what the message instructs him to do, he got the original qubit,$|\psi_c\rangle$. To explain more, Bob did not measure anything, he put his qubits through a binary gate, but the gate is unitary. Bob got his $|\psi_c\rangle$ after receiving two measly classical bits [39]. The Quantum Teleportation process: it starts with two entangled particles, generally identified as Alice and Bob. Additionally, Alice holds an additional particle called Charlie, meant to be teleportated to Bob. In this method, Alice makes a measurement involving her particle (Charlie) and the particle given for teleportation. Proceeding further, Alice executes a Bell measurement on her particles, gathering informations about the shared quantum state of the entangled particles—Alice's and Bob's; while avoiding direct measurement of their individual states. Following this, Alice uses classical communication to send the measurement result to Bob. The classical data comprises important characteristics about the original particle's quantum state. Afterwards, Bob, informed by Alice's classical knowledge, does certain quantum operations to his entangled particle. These operations bring about a transition in Bob's particle, aligning it with the initial state of Charlie. With this manipulation finished, Bob's particle successfully "mimics" the quantum state of the original particle, Charlie, eventually ending in the successful teleportation of its properties over space. Key Quantum Teleportation Protocols include the fundamental Original Protocol [40], which established the notion of quantum teleportation and proved the non-local transfer of quantum information. Additionally, the Dense Coding Protocol uses quantum teleportation principles to permit effective transfer of classical information via entangled particles. Cluster State Teleportation allows the teleportation of cluster states important in quantum computing, allowing distributed quantum computation. Finally, the Continuous Variable Teleportation protocol manages continuous quantum variables, such as quantum state phase and amplitude, allowing the development of high-capacity quantum communication channels.

5.5.1 Quantum teleportation implementation

Quantum teleportation depends on the manipulation of quantum states through the application of quantum gates, which are basic operations that affect the state of a quantum system. These gates play an important part in preparing, entangling, and affecting the particles involved in the teleportation process. Let us examine how quantum gates are applied in quantum teleportation using a simple example in Qiskit, a common framework for quantum computing. Let us consider that Alice want to send to Bob an unknown state using bell state as an entangled state (**Figure 17**).

The given Qiskit code generates and simulates a quantum circuit that includes many quantum gates and operations. We'll break down the code step by step to understand it (**Table 3**).

Beginning with the *Qasm* simulator, the code goes as follows: The code is written in Qiskit, a quantum computing tool, to simulate and show quantum circuit results using a specific quantum simulator. Let us investigate the code's parts and understand its purpose: To begin, the line "*simulator = Aer.getbackend(qasmsimulator)*" initializes a quantum simulator using Qiskit's Aer backend. The *qasmsimulator* backend simulates quantum circuit activity and estimates probability for different measurement results. Next, the code "*result = execute(circuit, backend = simulator).result()*" uses the "execute" function to run the quantum circuit on the provided simulator backend ("simulator"). After that, by using the "*.result()*" function, results can be obtained from the execution process. Moreover, the import phase here is "*from*

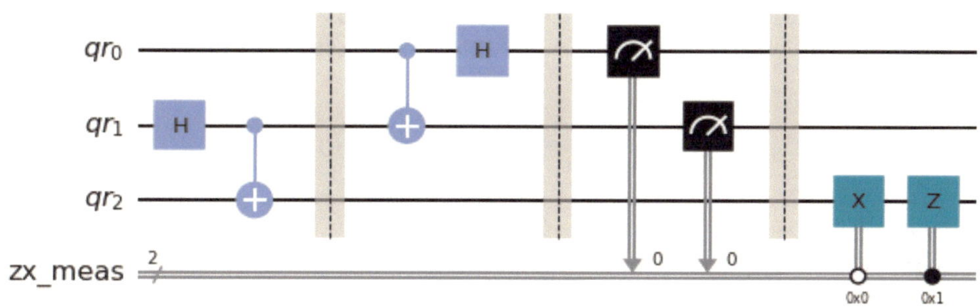

Figure 17.
Quantum teleportation circuit using bell state as entangled state.

Applications	Explanation
Importing Libraries	The code imports essential libraries
Quantum and Classical Registers	Registers for qubits and measurement.
Quantum Circuit Initialization	Called "circuit" formed with quantum and classical registers.
Hadamard Gate	Create a superposition between the qubits
Controlled-NOT Gate	CNOT gate entangles qubits; flips target if control qubit = 1
Barrier	separates circuit areas for improved clarity
Measurements	Qubits 0 and 1 measured, results in classical bits
X Gate and Z Gate	Conditional qubit operations based on classical measurements.

Table 3.
Explaining the use of the gate in the quantum circuit.

qiskit.tools.visualization import plothistogram" takes in the *plothistogram* use from Qiskit's visualization tools, allowing the creation of histograms that represent measurement results. In the end, the code provides a histogram plot using "*plothistogram*(*result.getcounts*(*circuit*))", offers a visual representation of the measurement results collected from the circuit performance. The *getcounts*(*circuit*) function obtains result counts, and the "$plot_h istogram$" tool shows these counts as a histogram. The second part of the algorithm includes determining outcome probabilities using the simulator (**Figures 18** and **19**).

The resultant probabilities obtained from the executed quantum circuit represent the possibility of measuring the states. The circuit, including qubit gates and operations, creates probabilities for measuring varied qubit states. Breaking down the results for 00 and 01 states: For 00, a probability of 0.497 corresponds to a 49.7 %, the probability of measuring both qubits in state $|0\rangle$. In the case of 01 the probability of 0.503 shows a 50.3 %, the possibility of measuring the first qubit in state $|0\rangle$ and the second qubit in state $|1\rangle$. These probabilities replicate the behavior of the quantum circuit, created by applied gates and operations. Guided by quantum physics, measurement outputs are fundamentally probabilistic, their probabilities depending on qubit states during measurement [41].

Similar behavior is seen in the Aer simulator, but with slightly different result of the outcome probability values. Next, we plot the *ibmqqasmsimulator* (**Figures 20–22**).

For the state 00, the probability is 0.512 is 51.2 %, the probability of measuring both qubits in the state $|0\rangle$. For the state 01, the probability is 0.488 is 48.8 %, the probability of measuring the first qubit in state $|0\rangle$ and the second qubit in state $|1\rangle$.

Comparing these results with the previous outcomes obtained from the Qasm simulator (for 00 with probability = 0.497, and for 01 with probability = 0.503) and

```
simulator = Aer.get_backend('qasm_simulator')
result = execute(circuit, backend = simulator).result()
from qiskit.tools.visualization import plot_histogram
plot_histogram(result.get_counts(circuit))
```

Figure 18.
Outcome probability code of Qasm simulator.

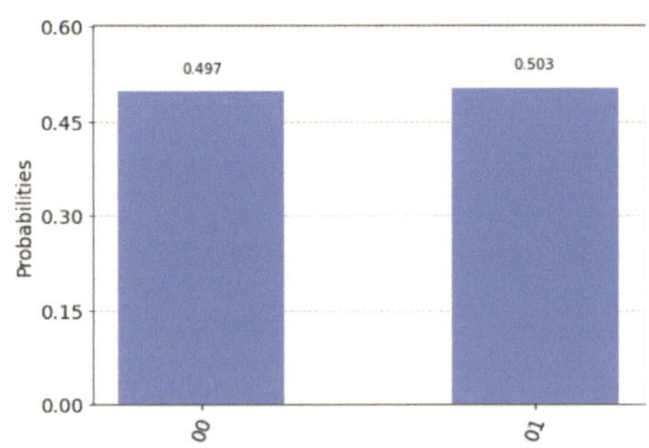

Figure 19.
Outcome probability of Qasm simulator.

```
simulator = Aer.get_backend('aer_simulator')
result = execute(circuit, backend = simulator).result()
from qiskit.tools.visualization import plot_histogram
plot_histogram(result.get_counts(circuit))
```

Figure 20.
Outcome probability code of Aer simulator.

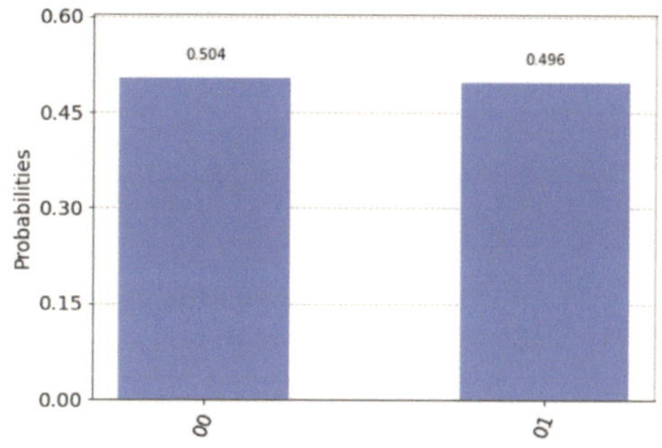

Figure 21.
Outcome probability of Aer simulator.

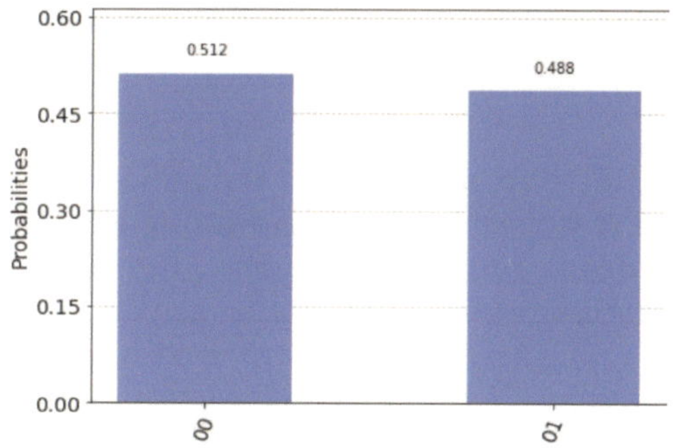

Figure 22.
Quantum teleportation circuit using bell state as entangled state.

the Aer simulator (for 00, probability = 0.504, and for 01, probability = 0.496), many observations can be made. The *ibmqqasmsimulator* has a different probability distribution, showing changes in quantum behavior compared to both the Qasm and Aer simulators. The particular probabilities associated with each state vary by the simulator being used, reflecting the random character of quantum systems. The advantages of using the *ibmqqasmsimulator* extend beyond basic result variations. This simulator is meant to exactly copy the behavior of real IBM Quantum devices, capturing real-world quantum effects and noise. Despite other idealistic simulators (such as the Qasm and Aer simulators), the *ibmqqasmsimulator* gives a more realistic simulation that matches the settings of quantum computers. This allows researchers and developers to examine how quantum algorithms and circuits will work on real machines, perhaps exposing problems that are possible due to noise and other non-ideal conditions. Therefore, the *ibmqqasmsimulator* serves as a helpful simulator for testing and improving quantum algorithms before deploying them on real quantum devices.

5.5.2 Bidirectional quantum teleportation (BQT) implementation

BQT is our approach includes the deployment of a Bell Quantum Teleporter (BQT), a conceptual construct that employs the quantum entanglement to perform teleportation by transferring two arbitrary quantum states in opposite directions. To assist this process, we use two pairs of Bell states, precisely prepared to encode and transport the quantum information. Furthermore, two Cluster states are brought forth, acting as the basic entangled states (**Figure 23**).

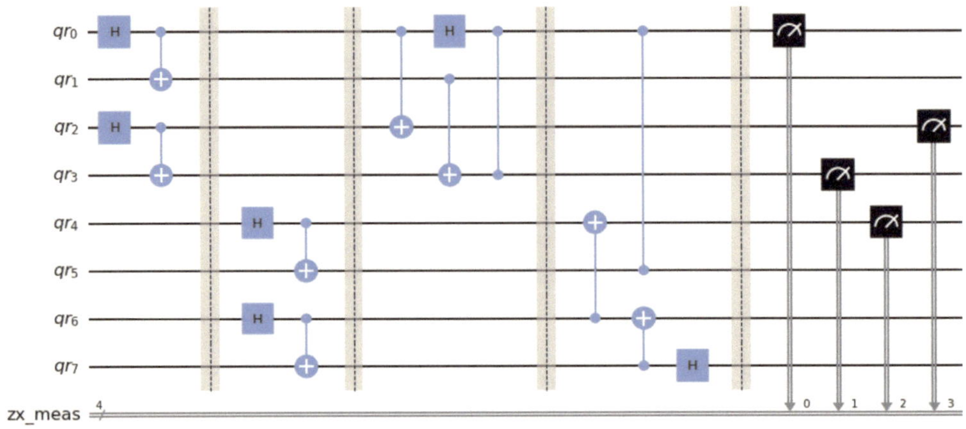

Figure 23.
Bidirectional quantum teleportation circuit using two bell states and two cluster states as entangled state.

The code initializes the Qiskit environment and builds a quantum circuit named "circuit" with 8 qubits and 4 classical bits for measurement results. The quantum and classical registers are defined using the QuantumRegister and ClassicalRegister classes, respectively. we establish two Bell states using Hadamard (H) gates and controlled-X (CX or CNOT) gates. Bell states are maximally entangled quantum states. The first two qubits (qr[0] and qr.[1]) constitute the first Bell state, while the following two qubits (qr[2] and qr.[3]) form the second Bell state. Then we generated two cluster states, which are different quantum states with a special entanglement structure. In this example, the cluster states are produced using Hadamard (H) gates and controlled-X (CX) gates. For the example presented, the cluster states are assumed to be $|00> + |11>$. After then quantum teleportation happens from qubit 0 (sender) to qubit 4 (receiver). It includes a series of controlled operations, including controlled-X (CX) gates and controlled-Z (CZ) gates. Quantum teleportation allows the teleportation of quantum information from one qubit to another using entanglement. Then we conduct another round of quantum teleportation, this time from qubit 4 back to qubit 0. Similar controlled methods are utilized to achieve this teleportation. We apply operations Measurements to qubits 0, 3, 4, and 2, which correspond to the transmitter and receiver qubits. The measurement results will be saved in the classical registers cr[0], cr[1], cr[2], and cr[3]. In our case, when we plot and simulate the circuit using QASM, Aer, and the Belem simulator, we obtain results that accurately describe the behavior of quantum teleportation and entanglement. Each simulator gives an individual perspective on how the quantum circuit operations establish, delivering significant information on the quantum states and measurement results. Here's what we observe (**Figure 24**).

The *Qasm* simulator emulates quantum processes using a classical way, to study the optimal behavior of quantum circuits. When plotted in the Qasm simulator, the circuit show a clear sequence of gate operations, entanglement, teleportation steps, and measurements. The measurement outputs are probabilistic, reflecting the quantum nature of the system, but the simulation is not account for noise that genuine quantum hardware. The Aer simulator gives a more realistic simulation by integrating noise models and other non-ideal factors. When our circuit is plotted in the *Aer* simulator, we detect further fluctuations in the measurement outputs because of simulated noise. This provide us information into how noise affects the teleportation

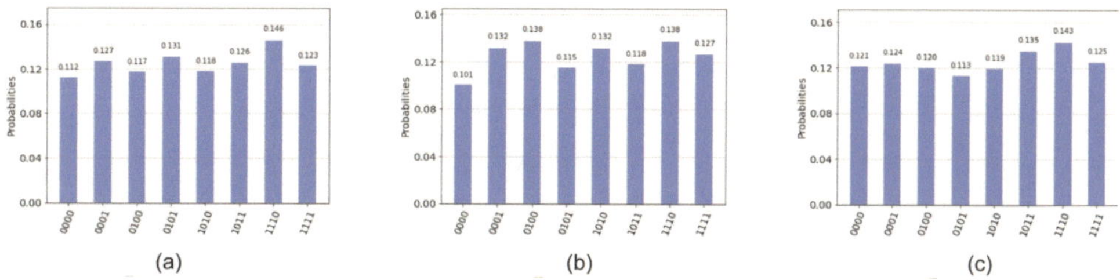

Figure 24.
Three separate quantum simulation perspectives: (a) the Aer simulator shows real-world noise affects, (b) the Qasm simulator reveals the ideal quantum teleportation process, and (c) the Belem simulator delivers advanced, high-fidelity insights.

process. The *Belem* simulator is especially built to deliver accurate quantum simulations using high-performance computer resources. When visualizing the circuit in the Belem simulator, we get an exact simulations that shows from the results a complicated interactions between qubits and complex noise models. This simulator provides us a complete knowledge of how the circuit operate on complex quantum systems, delivering insights into possible obstacles and improvements required for real-world implementation.

6. Closing remarks

From classical computation to quantum computation, we have begun on the possibility of changing our understanding of computing power and information processing. Through this study, we have exploited the power of quantum physics to show how we went from classical computers paradigm their challenges to quantum computing. By applying Qiskit platform, we managed to explain the basics of building a quantum teleportation circuit as an example, which has enabled us to experience quantum entanglement in action. Through precisely controlled procedures and measurable consequences, we have proven the teleportation of information between qubits, overcoming physical barriers in a manner that conventional communication could never do. In the context of bidirectional quantum teleportation, the difficulties of sending and receiving quantum states have been released, showing the complication of Bell states and cluster states that support this amazing phenomenon. Quantum computers interact and cooperate in ways that give us the results fast and more accurate. The achievements gained with Qiskit open the door for a quantum revolution that might influence industries ranging from encryption to optimization and drug discovery. By understanding the basic principles of quantum physics and applying the power of quantum gates and entanglement, we begin to find the transformational powers of quantum computers. With Qiskit as our guide, the road from classical to quantum computing becomes an exciting adventure in defining the future of technology and science.

Author details

Abdallah Slaoui[1,2*], Nada Ikken[1], Lalla Btissam Drissi[1,2,3] and Rachid Ahl Laamara[1,2]

1 LPHE-Modeling and Simulation, Faculty of Sciences, Mohammed V. University in Rabat, Rabat, Morocco

2 Centre of Physics and Mathematics, CPM, Faculty of Sciences, Mohammed V. University in Rabat, Rabat, Morocco

3 College of Physical and Chemical Sciences, Hassan II Academy of Sciences and Technology, Rabat, Morocco

*Address all correspondence to: abdallah.slaoui@um5s.net.ma

References

[1] Bremner MJ, Jozsa R, Shepherd DJ. Classical simulation of commuting quantum computations implies collapse of the polynomial hierarchy. Proceedings of the Royal Society A Mathematical, Physical and Engineering Sciences. 2011; **467**:459-472

[2] Montanaro A. Quantum algorithms: An overview. NPJ Quantum Information. 2016;**2**:1-8

[3] Aaronson S, Chen L. Complexity-theoretic foundations of quantum supremacy experiments. arXiv preprint arXiv:1612.05903. 2016

[4] Williams CP, Clearwater SH. Explorations in Quantum Computing. Santa Clara: Telos; 1998

[5] Knill E. Quantum computing. Nature. 2010;**463**:441-443

[6] Ladd TD, Jelezko F, Laflamme R, Nakamura Y, Monroe C, O'Brien JL. Quantum computing. Nature. 2010;**464**: 45-53

[7] Canteaut A, Videau M. Symmetric boolean functions. IEEE Transactions on Information Theory. 2005;**51**:2791-2811

[8] O'Donnell R. Some topics in analysis of Boolean functions. In: Proceedings of the Fortieth Annual ACM Symposium on Theory of Computing. 2008. pp. 569-578

[9] Steane A. Quantum computing. Reports on Progress in Physics. 1998;**61**: 117

[10] Steane A. Quantum computing. Reports on Progress in Physics. 1998; **61**:117

[11] Keyl M. Fundamentals of quantum information theory. Physics Reports. 2002;**369**:431-548

[12] DiVincenzo DP. Quantum computation. Science. 1995;**270**:255-261

[13] Aharonov D. Quantum computation. Annual Reviews of Computational Physics VI. 1999;**1999**:259-346

[14] Erdős L, Schlein B, Yau HT. Derivation of the cubic non-linear Schrödinger equation from quantum dynamics of many-body systems. Inventiones Mathematicae. 2007;**167**: 515-614

[15] Ollitrault PJ, Miessen A, Tavernelli I. Molecular quantum dynamics: A quantum computing perspective. Accounts of Chemical Research. 2021;**54**: 4229-4238

[16] Grover LK. Synthesis of quantum superpositions by quantum computation. Physical Review Letters. 2000;**85**:1334

[17] Khrennikov A. Roots of quantum computing supremacy: Superposition, entanglement, or complementarity? European Physical Journal Special Topics. 2021;**230**:1053-1057

[18] Preskill J. Quantum computing and the entanglement frontier. arXiv preprint:1203.5813. 2012

[19] Sørensen A, Mølmer K. Entanglement and quantum computation with ions in thermal motion. Physical Review A. 2000; **62**:022311

[20] Raussendorf R, Wei TC. Quantum computation by local measurement. Annual Review of Condensed Matter Physics. 2012;**3**:239-261

[21] Patera J, Zassenhaus H. The Pauli matrices in n dimensions and finest

gradings of simple lie algebras of type a n–1. Journal of Mathematical Physics. 1988;**29**:665-673

[22] Briegel HJ, Browne DE, Dür W, Raussendorf R, Van den Nest M. Measurement-based quantum computation. Nature Physics. 2009;**5**: 19-26

[23] Mosseri R, Dandoloff R. Geometry of entangled states, Bloch spheres and Hopf fibrations. Journal of Physics A: Mathematical and General. 2001;**34**: 10243

[24] Mäkelä H, Messina A. N-qubit states as points on the Bloch sphere. Physica Scripta. 2010;**2010**:014054

[25] Yu CH, Gao F, Lin S, Wang J. Quantum data compression by principal component analysis. Quantum Information Processing. 2019;**18**:1-20

[26] Legeza Ö, Sólyom J. Quantum data compression, quantum information generation, and the density-matrix renormalization group method. Physical Review B. 2004;**70**:205118

[27] Dilip R, Liu YJ, Smith A, Pollmann F. Data compression for quantum machine learning. Physical Review Research. 2022;**4**:043007

[28] Gisin N, Ribordy G, Tittel W, Zbinden H. Quantum cryptography. Reviews of Modern Physics. 2002;**74**:145

[29] Zhang Q, Yin J, Chen TY, Lu S, Zhang J, Li XQ, et al. Experimental fault-tolerant quantum cryptography in a decoherence-free subspace. Physical Review A. 2006;**73**:020301

[30] Bennett CH, Brassard G, Ekert AK. Quantum cryptography. Scientific American. 1992;**267**:50-57

[31] Shor PW, Preskill J. Simple proof of security of the BB84 quantum key distribution protocol. Physical Review Letters. 2000;**85**:441

[32] Bennett CH, DiVincenzo DP. Quantum information and computation. Nature. 2000;**404**:247-255

[33] Jaeger G. Quantum Information. New York: Springer; 2007. pp. 81-89

[34] Harrow A, Hayden P, Leung D. Superdense coding of quantum states. Physical Review Letters. 2004;**92**:187901

[35] Zhao J, Jeng H, Conlon LO, Tserkis S, Shajilal B, Liu K, et al. Enhancing quantum teleportation efficacy with noiseless linear amplification. Nature Communications. 2023;**14**:4745

[36] Mafi Y, Kazemikhah P, Ahmadkhaniha A, Aghababa H, Kolahdouz M. Bidirectional quantum teleportation of an arbitrary number of qubits over a noisy quantum system using 2n bell states as quantum channel. Optical and Quantum Electronics. 2022; **54**:568

[37] Kirdi ME, Slaoui A, Hadfi HE, Daoud M. Improving the probabilistic quantum teleportation efficiency of arbitrary superposed coherent state using multipartite even and odd j-spin coherent states as resource. Applied Physics B. 2023;**129**:94

[38] Kirdi ME, Slaoui A, Hadfi HE, Daoud M. Efficient quantum controlled teleportation of an arbitrary three-qubit state using two GHZ entangled states and one bell entangled state. Journal of Russian Laser Research. 2023;**44**:121-134

[39] Legeza Ö, Sólyom J. Optimizing the density-matrix renormalization group method using quantum information

entropy. Physical Review B. 2003;**68**: 195116

[40] Bennett CH, Brassard G, Crépeau C, Jozsa R, Peres A, Wootters WK. Teleporting an unknown quantum state via dual classical and Einstein-Podolsky-Rosen channels. Physical Review Letters. 1993;**70**:1895

[41] Ikken N, Slaoui A, Laamara RA, Drissi LB. Bidirectional quantum teleportation of even and odd coherent states through the multipartite Glauber coherent state: Theory and implementation. arXiv preprint: 2306.00505. 2023

Chapter 3

Quantification of Entanglement

Bilal Benzimoun and Abdelali Sajia

Abstract

Quantum entanglement, a fundamental concept in quantum physics, has been elucidated through the development of Bell's inequalities. Recent advancements have enabled controlled manipulation and measurement of entangled quantum states. This chapter provides a concise overview of entanglement's mathematical underpinnings, its manipulation, and quantification. Special attention is given to quantification methods and their implications in quantum information. Key principles and measures are presented to facilitate a foundational understanding. Readers are encouraged to supplement this overview with comprehensive review articles and primary literature for further insights.

Keywords: quantum entanglement, Bell's inequalities, non-locality, quantum correlations, separability, quantification

1. Introduction

The idea of entanglement has been immensely significant in shaping the progress of quantum physics. Initially, it was clear that the qualitative characteristic of quantum theory distinguishes itself strikingly from our classical intuition. The subsequent development of an idea conceived by John Stewart Bell, known as Bell's inequalities, allowed for a quantitative distinction and the construction of a non-localized characteristic of quantum theory that could be experimentally verified. Bell's inequalities can be seen as an attempt to quantify the quantum correlations responsible for the counterintuitive features of entangled states [1]. At that time, it was nearly unimaginable that such quantum correlations could be created between different quantum systems. However, progress made in recent years has provided more opportunities to prepare such states coherently, manipulate and measure individual quantum systems, and create controllable quantum correlations.

Given the new status of the subject, it is entirely natural and important to uncover the mathematical structures underlying its theoretical description. We are interested in questions such as the nature of entanglement, including its characterization, manipulation, and quantification.

In the following, we aim to provide an overview summarizing the results obtained within the framework of these three questions. We will place particular emphasis on developments regarding the quantification of entanglement. We will discuss the motivation behind the study of these quantum correlations while presenting their implications in the development of quantum information. We present the underlying basic principles of the theory and the main results, including numerous useful entanglement measures, as well as explicit formulas. We hope that this chapter will give the reader a good initial impression of the subject and enable them to approach the next chapter more easily, as well as the abundant literature on this topic. Of course, as in any work of this kind, it is inevitable that we have made several omissions in this process. We, therefore, encourage the interested reader to explore various other interesting review articles (for example, Refs. [2–7]) and, of course, the original literature.

2. Basic properties of entanglement

What is entanglement?—Any study of entanglement must begin with a discussion of what entanglement is and how we use it. In what follows, we will adopt a highly operational viewpoint. Then, the usefulness of entanglement becomes apparent as it allows us to overcome a specific constraint that we will soon refer to as the Local Operations and Classical Communication (LOCC) constraint—a term we will explain shortly. This restriction has both technological and fundamental motivations and naturally arises in many explicit physical contexts involving remote quantum communication [8, 9].

2.1 Quantum operations

Within the realm of quantum mechanics, a formal mathematical framework is employed to elucidate a wide spectrum of transformations that a quantum system can potentially undergo. The inception of the concept of a generalized stochastic transformation applied to a density matrix is attributed to George Sudarshan. This formalism, referred to as quantum operations, extends its purview beyond the confines of unitary temporal evolution and symmetry alterations of isolated systems. It encompasses the intricate ramifications of measurements and transient interactions with an encompassing environment. In the domain of quantum computing, the nomenclature "quantum operation" is interchangeably employed to denote what is also recognized as a "quantum channel" [10].

It should be noted that within the literature, certain authors ascribe a more specific meaning to the term "quantum operation," using it to specifically denote completely positive (CP) and trace-non-increasing mappings operating on the space of density matrices. Conversely, the term "quantum channel" is reserved for those within this subset that uphold strict trace preservation [11].

The formulation of quantum operations is contingent upon the elucidation of the density operator characterizing a quantum mechanical system. With rigor, a quantum operation is characterized as a linear, completely positive mapping from the ensemble of density operators to itself. In the context of quantum information, an additional constraint is often imposed upon a quantum operation denoted as ε, mandating its adherence to the notion of physicality, wherein $0 \leq \mathrm{Tr}[\varepsilon\rho] \leq 1$ is upheld for any state ρ.

Notably, certain quantum processes elude encapsulation within the framework of quantum operations. In principle, the density matrix of a quantum system retains the capacity for entirely arbitrary temporal evolution. The generality of quantum operations finds its augmentation in the concept of quantum instruments, which not only encompass quantum information but also assimilate classical information gleaned during measurement processes.

2.1.1 Quantum operations on the state of a single qubit

The expression of a singular qubit's state can be formally articulated as follows:

$$|\psi\rangle = \alpha|0\rangle + \beta|1\rangle, \tag{1}$$

where α and β are intricate complex coefficients. The quantum state $|\psi\rangle$ can be interpreted as a vector in the Hilbert space, denoted as:

$$|\psi\rangle = (\alpha \ \ \beta). \tag{2}$$

It is worth noting that due to the principle of probability conservation, specifically $|\alpha|^2 + |\beta|^2 = 1$, and the inherent insensitivity to the global phase, merely two real parameters are sufficient to characterize a distinct quantum state of a single qubit. This characteristic is articulated through the following expression:

$$|\psi\rangle = \cos\frac{\theta}{2}|0\rangle + \sin\frac{\theta}{2}e^{i\phi}|1\rangle, \tag{3}$$

where $0 \le \phi \le 2\pi$ and $0 \le \theta \le \pi$. This signifies an unequivocal correspondence between qubit states ($\mathbb{C}^2$) and points situated on the surface of a unit sphere ($\mathbb{R}^3$). This geometric connection is more elaborated upon in the initial section as the Bloch sphere representation of a one-qubit state [12].

Quantum operations are conventionally delineated through matrices. A quantum operation performed on a qubit is symbolized by a unitary matrix U with dimensions 2×2. The operation's effect on the quantum state is executed by matrix–vector multiplication, viz.:

$$|\psi'\rangle = U|\psi\rangle. \tag{4}$$

A general unitary matrix is anticipated to transform $|\psi\rangle$ into the aforementioned state. This is described by the unitary matrix:

$$U = \begin{pmatrix} \cos(\theta/2) & a \\ e^{i\phi}\sin\theta/2 & b \end{pmatrix}, \tag{5}$$

where a and b are intricate complex variables, constrained by the condition $U^\dagger U = 1\!\!1$ for all $0 \le \theta \le \pi$. This specification results in three constraints, ultimately leading to the expressions $a \to -e^{i\lambda}\sin\theta/2$ and $b \to e^{i\lambda+i\phi}\cos\theta/2$, where $0 \le \lambda \le 2\pi$.

The comprehensive form of the unitary matrix, adhering to these constraints, takes the shape:

$$U = \begin{pmatrix} \cos(\theta/2) & -e^{i\lambda}\sin\theta/2 \\ e^{i\phi}\sin\theta/2 & e^{i\lambda+i\phi}\cos\theta/2 \end{pmatrix}. \tag{6}$$

Evidently, this emerges as the most comprehensive manifestation of a unitary matrix for a qubit, taking into account all pertinent considerations.

2.1.2 Multi-qubit operations

The space of a quantum computer grows exponentially with the number of qubits. For n qubits, the complex vector space is of dimension $d = 2^n$. To describe the states of a multi-qubit system, the tensor product is used to "combine" operators and basic vectors.

Let us start by considering a two-qubit system. Given that two operators A and B act individually on qubits, the co-operator $A \otimes B$ acting on two qubits is

$$A \otimes B = \begin{pmatrix} A_{00}\begin{pmatrix} B_{00} & B_{01} \\ B_{10} & B_{11} \end{pmatrix} & A_{01}\begin{pmatrix} B_{00} & B_{01} \\ B_{10} & B_{11} \end{pmatrix} \\ A_{10}\begin{pmatrix} B_{00} & B_{01} \\ B_{10} & B_{11} \end{pmatrix} & A_{11}\begin{pmatrix} B_{00} & B_{01} \\ B_{10} & B_{11} \end{pmatrix} \end{pmatrix} \tag{7}$$

where A_{jk} and B_{lm} are, respectively, the elements of matrices A and B.

Similarly, the basis vectors for the two-qubit system are formed using the tensor product of the basis vectors for a single qubit.

3. Entanglement

Entanglement arises from the application of the principle of superposition to a composite system comprising multiple subsystems, typically two in the context under consideration. Each of these subsystems is analogous to an individual particle. Let us consider a scenario where we have two particles, denoted as Particle 1 and Particle 2. Particle 1 is associated with two mutually exclusive states, namely state A and state C, representing conflicting attributes such as disparate spatial positions or divergent energy levels. Conversely, Particle 2 can exist in either state B or state D, similarly embodying contradictory properties, such as occupying distinct spatial coordinates. The composite state denoted as AB emerges as a product state, signifying that Particle 1 occupies state A while Particle 2 occupies state B. Correspondingly, state CD indicates that Particle 1 assumes state C and Particle 2 adopts state D.

Now, the amalgamation of states AB and CD into a superposition, denoted as AB + CD, results from the application of the principle of superposition to the entire bipartite system. This combined state, referred to as an entangled state, distinctly manifests the characteristics of superposition, thereby evading the ascription of definite attributes to the individual particles. Unlike the product states AB and CD, which endow specific attributes to Particle 1 and Particle 2 (e.g., Particle 1 is localized at position A while Particle 2 resides at position B), the entangled state encapsulates a lack of such determinacy. Instead, it signifies a nexus between potentialities pertaining to Particle 1 and Particle 2, whereby their states exhibit correlation. Concretely, upon conducting measurements, if Particle 1 assumes state A, Particle 2 unequivocally occupies state B, and conversely, when Particle 1 is in state C, Particle 2 correspondingly resides in state D.

In essence, the entanglement of Particles 1 and 2 implies a fundamental interdependence, where the characterization of one particle necessitates reference to the other. This distinctive attribute persists even when the individual attributes of Particle 1 and Particle 2 can be independently discerned within the framework of the product states AB or CD, but not within the context of the superposition AB + CD. It is the superposition of these two product states that engenders the phenomenon of entanglement.

The prevailing consensus underscores the necessity of adopting a quantum description, rather than a classical one, at the fundamental level of nature [13]. Nevertheless, a comprehensive comprehension of the profound implications and ramifications of this proposition remains an intricate endeavor. Particularly noteworthy is the paradigm shift engendered by the transition from the classical phase space concept to the abstract Hilbert space framework, which becomes salient in the context of composite systems. To elucidate this, we consider a multipartite system comprising n constituent subsystems. In the classical depiction, the aggregate state space of this system comprises the Cartesian product of the individual state spaces of the n subsystems, implying that the overall state invariably emerges as a product state of these n distinct systems. In stark contrast, in the quantum formalism, the collective Hilbert space H assumes the form of a tensor product of the individual subsystem spaces, denoted as $H = \otimes_{l=1}^{n} H_l$. In light of the principle of superposition, the collective state of the system can be expressed as follows:

$$|\psi\rangle = \sum_{\mathbf{n}} c_n |\mathbf{i}_n\rangle \tag{8}$$

Here, $\mathbf{i}_n = i_1, i_2, \ldots, i_n$ signifies a multi-index, and $|\mathbf{i}_n\rangle = |i_1\rangle \otimes |i_2\rangle \otimes \ldots \otimes |i_n\rangle$ denotes a multipartite state that, in general, defies representation as a mere product of the individual subsystem states $|\psi\rangle \neq \; |\psi_1\rangle \otimes |\psi_2\rangle \otimes \ldots \otimes |\psi_n\rangle$.

Consequently, it becomes apparent that assigning an individual state vector to any one of the n subsystems without perturbing the others becomes, for the most part, an infeasible proposition. This formalizes the entanglement phenomenon, wherein the composite state exhibits an entwined nature that transcends classical superposition and facilitates the construction of exponential superpositions with a linear allocation of physical resources. This underpins the foundation for executing tasks that elude classical approaches.

In empirical applications, mixed states tend to be encountered more frequently than pure states. A mixed state of n entangled systems is characterized by its inability to be expressed as a convex combination of product states:

$$\rho \neq \sum_{i} p_i \rho_1^i \otimes \rho_2^i \otimes \ldots \otimes \rho_n^i \tag{9}$$

States that adhere to this definition of separability are termed "separable." Discerning whether a given state is separable or entangled based solely on the definition itself proves challenging in practice. Thus, the predicament of determining separability, known as the separability problem, stands as a fundamental inquiry regarding entanglement. Notably, an alternative interpretation of "Entangled States" has recently emerged, characterizing such states as those beyond the scope of simulation through classical correlations [14]. This novel perspective conceptualizes entanglement in terms of state behavior rather than state preparation.

For bipartite systems, wherein the Hilbert space $H = H_1 \otimes H_2$ and $dimH_1 = dimH_2 = 2$, the states $|\psi^{\pm}\rangle$ and $|\phi^{\pm}\rangle$, sometimes referred to as EPR (Einstein-Podolsky-Rosen) states, demonstrate remarkable attributes [15]. Notably, upon measuring one subsystem, an outcome of either $|0\rangle$ or $|1\rangle$ is equally probable. However, the measurement outcomes of the two subsystems exhibit perfect correlation.

This facet, as delineated by Schrödinger, underscores the profound uncertainty surrounding the individual subsystems, despite possessing complete knowledge of the entire system due to its pure-state nature.

To date, prevalent sources of entanglement commonly involve entangled photon states engendered through negative-type I or type II nonlinear parametric processes, yielding pairs of entangled photons from downconversion. These pairs exhibit matching or orthogonal polarizations [16]. This process, notably, facilitates the creation of an entangled basis within the Bell state. Moreover, a diverse array of alternative sources of entangled quantum systems exists, encompassing entangled photon pairs originating from calcium atoms [17], entangled ions prepared in electromagnetic Paul traps [18] entangled atoms in quantum electrodynamic cavities [19], enduring entanglement among macroscopic atomic ensembles [20, 21], entangled microwave photons from quantum dots [22], entanglement among nuclear spins in individual molecules [23], and entanglement bridging atomic and optical ensembles [24].

3.1 Local manipulation of an entangled quantum state (LOCC)

One of the paramount procedures within the realm of quantum information entails the distillation or concentration of entanglement inherent to a given quantum state. This endeavor fundamentally encompasses two distinct categories of protocols. The initial category relies on non-local quantum measurements executed on multiple replicas of the primary quantum state. The second category involves exclusively local operations, supplemented by the prospect of classical communication (referred to as LOCC), enacted upon a sole instance of the quantum state. Hence, these protocols hold distinct allure from an empirical standpoint, given that local measurements can be feasibly conducted in contrast to their non-local counterparts.

From the vantage point of quantum communication, the significance of LOCC protocols becomes evident due to the absence of impeccably efficient communication channels in real-world scenarios. Consequently, it becomes pertinent to contemplate the extent of entanglement achievable from imperfectly entangled states that arise, for instance, during the dissemination of an ideally entangled state between two observers employing solely LOCC mechanisms (as expounded in Chitambar et al. [25]).

In the context of the foundational inquiries intrinsic to quantum information theory, which encompass pursuits such as the comprehensive comprehension and characterization of entanglement, LOCC operations assume a pivotal role by virtue of their intrinsic attributes. As the concept of entanglement intimately hinges upon non-local characteristics of a physical state, LOCC operations are inherently incapable of altering the inherent essence of entanglement. By harnessing this classification of operation, it becomes possible to delineate disparate sets of equivalent states, exemplified by entities like the “W” or “GHZ” states. Instances representative of each category can be applied within experimental settings to fulfill analogous tasks, albeit with varying probabilities.

Elucidating the physical processes underpinning LOCC operations can be facilitated through contemplation of a rudimentary illustration. Envision a scenario wherein two observers, namely Alice and Bob, partake in the mutual possession of two Bell states.

$$|\Phi^-\rangle = \frac{1}{\sqrt{2}}(|0\rangle_A|0\rangle_B - |1\rangle_A|1\rangle_B) \tag{10}$$

$$|\Psi^-\rangle = \frac{1}{\sqrt{2}}(|0\rangle_A|1\rangle_B - |1\rangle_A|0\rangle_B) \tag{11}$$

In the context of quantum communication, Alice and Bob share a traditional communication channel, which could be a telephone or the Internet. Within this framework, they possess a choice between two jointly held quantum states, the specific identity of which remains undisclosed to them. Through the utilization of Local Operations and Classical Communication (LOCC), Alice and Bob are empowered to differentiate between these two states. This is accomplished by Alice executing a measurement on her quantum bit (qubit) and conveying the measurement outcome to Bob. Subsequently, Bob performs a measurement on his qubit. These actions culminate in the definitive identification of the shared state. To illustrate, in an instance where Alice measures the state $|0\rangle$ and Bob measures $|1\rangle$, they ascertain that the state in question is $|\Psi^-\rangle$.

At the heart of LOCC protocols lies the pursuit of attaining a maximal entangled state relative to an entanglement measurement, such as entanglement formation. The LOCC protocol for a two-qubit scenario can be represented as a mapping:

$$\rho' = \frac{A \otimes B\rho A^\dagger \otimes B^\dagger}{Tr\left(A \otimes B\rho A^\dagger \otimes B^\dagger\right)} \tag{12}$$

Wherein, the factors $AA^\dagger$ and $BB^\dagger$ are constrained to be less than or equal to unity, and $Tr\left(A \otimes B\rho A^\dagger \otimes B^\dagger\right)$ denotes the success probability of the protocol. The local operations A and B can be expressed as:

$$A = U_A \begin{pmatrix} \alpha_1 & 0 \\ 0 & \alpha_2 \end{pmatrix} U'_A \tag{13}$$

Here, the unitary transformations U_A and $U'A$ are unitary matrices, and the parameters $\alpha 1,2$ adhere to the range $0 \leq \alpha_{1,2} \leq 1$. It is also stipulated that the set of operations represented by A is invertible.

Examination of the most comprehensive protocol, encompassing mixed states in the final state composition, is deemed unnecessary, given that mixing tends to diminish the monotonically valued property of entanglement.

Initiating from a given mixed state ρ, characterized by non-zero entanglement of formation, and employing a LOCC protocol, a transformed state ρ' can be realized, embodying maximal entanglement of formation. This transformed state ρ' conforms to a distinctive structure, referred to as the Diagonal Bell state:

$$\rho' r_1, r_2, r_3 = \frac{1}{4}\left(\mathbf{1} + \sum i = 1^3 r_i \sigma_i \otimes \sigma_i\right) \tag{14}$$

Here, the coefficients r_i all possess the same sign, with the ordering $r_1 \leq r_2 \leq r_3$. The character of the diagonal Bell state remains invariant under local unitary transformations and offers an elucidation of entanglement density matrices that are locally equivalent.

It is noteworthy that Local Operations and Classical Communication (LOCC) applied to mixed states draws a parallel to Lorentz transformations in the realm of physics. By virtue of this correspondence, it can be deduced that there exist two distinct classes of all two-qubit states, susceptible to transformation into each other through LOCC operations. The first class entails states that can be transformed into the diagonal Bell form while preserving the rank of the density matrix. The second class comprises states that can be transformed into the diagonal Bell form with an asymptotically lower rank, indicative of separable states.

4. Operational approach

In continuation of our discourse concerning quantum operations and their inherent confinement to operations denoted as LOCC (Local Operations and Classical Communication), we are now poised to establish several tenets and fundamental definitions pertaining to entangled states. Given the extensive spectrum of tasks amenable to exploitation through entanglement, one could contemplate delineating entanglement employing an operational framework, wherein entanglement becomes the property harnessed within such protocols. Nevertheless, it is noteworthy that a diverse array of tasks of this nature exists, encompassing an assortment of conceivable measures of accomplishment. As a result, scenarios are likely to emerge wherein a state ρ_1 surpasses another state ρ_2 in efficacy for a particular task, while conversely, ρ_2 outperforms ρ_1 for a distinct task. Consequently, employing a task-centric approach for quantifying entanglement is liable to yield a multifaceted panorama rather than a singularly unified standpoint. Notwithstanding this intricacy, it remains feasible to delineate specific overarching principles that retain their validity irrespective of one's favored mode of entanglement utilization, provided that the ensemble of admissible operations corresponds to the LOCC category. This framework shall serve as our compass for embarking upon the quantification of entanglement. As such, we shall proceed to expound upon a subset of these postulates in a comprehensive manner:

- No entanglement in separable states

A state $\rho_{ABC...}$ of multiple parts $A, B, C, ...$ is called separable if it can be written in the form

$$\rho_{ABC...} = \sum_i p_i \rho_A^i \otimes \rho_B^i \otimes \rho_C^i \otimes ... \tag{15}$$

In the context of quantum systems, denoted by the probability distribution p_i, it is feasible to construct a particular quantum state through Local Operations and Classical Communication (LOCC) operations in a straightforward manner. Specifically, Alice, the central agent, selects a sample from the probability distribution p_i and promptly communicates this outcome to all other parties involved. Subsequently, each party represented as X independently generates a quantum state denoted as ρ_X^i that corresponds to the sampled outcome i while simultaneously erasing any information pertaining to the specific outcome i.

Because these quantum states can be generated exclusively through LOCC operations, they inherently conform to a framework compatible with a Local Hidden Variable (LHV) model, thereby permitting a classical description of all their correlations. Consequently, it is reasonable to assert that separable quantum states exhibit no entanglement within their inherent structure.

- All entangled states allow certain tasks to be performed better than LOCC

A "negative" definition of entanglement has been employed by the quantum information community, where entangled states are essentially those that can only be produced through LOCC (Local Operations and Classical Communication). Conversely, it can be demonstrated that a quantum state denoted as ρ can be perfectly generated using LOCC if and only if it is separable.

- Entanglement does not increase under LOCC transformations

Considering that LOCC-type operators have the capability to exclusively produce separable states rather than entangled ones, it follows that LOCC is incapable of engendering entanglement from a separable state. Assuming that we possess the knowledge that a quantum state denoted as ρ can be definitively transformed into another quantum state σ through LOCC operations, any outcomes attainable with σ and LOCC operations are also feasible with ρ and LOCC operations. Consequently, the entanglement level of quantum states remains unaltered or reduced by LOCC operations [9, 26, 27]. Thus, we can assert that ρ possesses, at the very least, the same degree of entanglement as σ.

- Entanglement remains unchanged under Local Unitary Operations

This characteristic arises as a consequence of the preceding property, as the reversibility of local unitary operations implies that states connected by local unitaries possess an equivalent level of entanglement. Consequently, in accordance with the principle of entanglement non-increase under LOCC, these two states maintain an equal degree of entanglement.

- Perfectly entangled states do indeed exist

We now possess an understanding of entangled states, with the ability to, in specific instances, determine the extent of entanglement between states. This naturally leads to the question of whether a maximally entangled state exists, one that surpasses all others in complexity. This assertion holds true, particularly in the context of bipartite systems consisting of two subsystems. It has been established that any locally equivalent pure state can be transformed into a locally equivalent maximally entangled pure state.

Mathematically, a maximally entangled pure state can be represented as:

$$|\psi_d^+\rangle = \frac{1}{\sqrt{d}}(|0,0\rangle + |1,1\rangle + \ldots + |d-1,d-1\rangle) \tag{16}$$

This claim is firmly supported, as we will illustrate in the subsequent sections, by the fact that any pure or mixed state within bipartite systems can be deterministically generated exclusively through the utilization of Local Operations and Classical Communication (LOCC) operations originating from maximally entangled states. This disparity in multipartite systems, where an equivalent statement is lacking, significantly adds to the complexities encountered when formulating an entanglement theory for such systems.

The considerations mentioned above have delineated the boundaries of entanglement. When we adopt LOCC (Local Operations and Classical Communication) as our set of permissible operations, separable states exhibit no entanglement, and we can identify specific states with maximum entanglement. These considerations also hint at the possibility of establishing a certain order. We can assert that one quantum state, denoted as ρ, is more entangled than another state, denoted as σ, if we can transform ρ into σ using LOCC operations. A pivotal question arises: Does this method yield a partial or complete ordering? To address this query, we need to ascertain the conditions under which a quantum state can be transformed into another through LOCC operations. Before delving into a discussion of entanglement measures, we will delve deeper into this inquiry in the subsequent section. It's worth noting that the idea that "entanglement does not increase under LOCC" is inherently linked to our confinement of quantum operations to LOCC; if other constraints apply with varying degrees of stringency, our concept of "perfect entanglement" will likewise evolve accordingly.

4.1 Manipulating a bipartite state

In the preceding section, it was mentioned that within bipartite systems, there exists a concept of maximally entangled states that remains independent of the particular measure of entanglement employed. This characteristic arises from the presence of perfectly entangled states, which have the unique property of being able to generate all other states solely through Local Operations and Classical Communication (LOCC). In the context of a two-qubit system, we shall observe that the most entangled states are those that are unitarily equivalent to the state described as:

$$|\psi_2^+\rangle = \frac{1}{\sqrt{2}}(|0,0\rangle + |1,1\rangle) \tag{17}$$

Our present objective is to substantiate this assertion by illustrating that for any pure bipartite state represented in the Schmidt decomposition form [28].

$$|\phi\rangle = \alpha|0,0\rangle + \beta|1,1\rangle \tag{18}$$

We have the capability to discover an LOCC (Local Operations and Classical Communication) protocol that reliably converts $|\psi_2^+\rangle$ into $|\phi\rangle$. This can be accomplished by providing an expression for the Kraus operators.

$$A_0 = (\alpha|0\rangle\ \langle 0| + \beta|1\rangle\ \langle 1|) \otimes \mathbf{1} \tag{19}$$

$$A_1 = (\alpha|0\rangle\ \langle 1| + \beta\ |1\rangle\ \langle 0|) \otimes (|1\rangle\ \langle 0| +\ |0\rangle\ \langle 1|) \tag{20}$$

Given $A_0^\dagger A_0 + A_1^\dagger A_1 = \mathbf{1} \otimes \mathbf{1}$ and $A_i|\psi\rangle = p_i|\phi\rangle$, then $|\phi\rangle\ \langle\phi| = A_0|\psi\rangle\ \langle\psi|A_0^\dagger + A_1|\psi\rangle\ \langle\psi|A_1^\dagger$. It is educational to examine the process of constructing this operation solely through LOCC transformations. To begin, we introduce an ancilla in the state 0 to Alice, resulting in the following state:

$$\frac{|00\rangle_A|0\rangle_B + |01\rangle_A|1\rangle_B}{\sqrt{2}}. \tag{21}$$

If we then perform the local unitary operation $|00\rangle \to \alpha\ |00\rangle + \beta\ |11\rangle$; $|01\rangle \to \alpha|10\rangle + \beta|01\rangle$ on Alice's two particles, we obtain:

$$\frac{|0\rangle_A(\alpha|00\rangle_{AB} + \beta|11\rangle_{AB}) + |1\rangle_A(\alpha|10\rangle_{AB} + \beta|01\rangle_{AB})}{\sqrt{2}} \tag{22}$$

Ultimately, a measurement conducted on Alice's ancillary particle within the local context produces two potential results. Should Alice measure $|0\rangle$, this information is promptly communicated to Bob, obviating the necessity for any additional actions on his part. Conversely, if Alice's measurement yields $|1\rangle$, Bob is required to implement a

σ_x operation on his particle. In both scenarios, the resulting outcome is the desired state expressed as $\alpha|00\rangle AB + \beta|11\rangle AB$. Given our ability to deterministically derive any arbitrary pure state from the initial state $|\psi_2^+\rangle$, we also possess the capability to generate any mixed state ρ.

4.2 Entanglement of formation

The concept of entanglement of formation quantifies entanglement in bipartite quantum states, as outlined in Ref. [29]. This measurement is defined as follows:

$$E_f(\rho) = min\, _E p_i E_E(|\psi_i\rangle) \tag{23}$$

The minimization is performed over the set of all pure states denoted as $E = (p_i, |\psi_i\rangle)$ that can represent the state $\rho = \sum_i p_i |\psi_i\rangle\ \langle\psi_i|$, where $E_E(|\psi\rangle)$ stands for the entanglement entropy defined for pure states. This particular extension of a quantity originally defined for pure states to mixed states is referred to as the "convex roof construction."

The entanglement of formation measures the quantity of Bell states required per copy in order to prepare multiple copies of ρ using a specific LOCC procedure:

- Choose a pure state, denoted as $|\phi_i\rangle$, to be generated from a probability distribution represented by q_i for every copy.

- To generate the necessary quantity of copies from Bell states for each distinct $|\phi_i\rangle$ state, follow these steps.

- Ignore details regarding the specific purity state of each copy.

4.3 Entanglement distillation

The effective dissemination of entanglement among remote entities is a vital prerequisite for various quantum information applications. Nonetheless, the fragility of entanglement poses a formidable challenge in shielding entangled states from decoherence-related disruptions, thus substantially affecting the efficiency of communication protocols. This is where entanglement distillation plays a pivotal role, enabling the augmentation of entanglement levels among communicating parties. This enhancement has emerged as a critical component in the realization of numerous quantum communication protocols.

The concept of entanglement distillation was originally introduced in Refs. [30, 31] with the aim of concentrating and refining entanglement resources, thereby enabling quantum communication protocols to function effectively in the presence of noise, as described in Bennett and Wooters [31]. Entanglement distillation is a process that involves two parties sharing n copies of a bipartite entangled state, during which specific LOCC (Local Operations and Classical Communication) procedures are executed to maximize the yield of maximally entangled state pairs, denoted as $k(n) \leq n$. In the limit of a large number of copies n, the asymptotic ratio k/n is referred to as the distillable entanglement, serving as a quantification of the amount of pure-state entanglement that can be extracted from a given state ρ.

The determination of whether a bipartite state ρ is distillable or not has been greatly simplified by the following criterion: A bipartite state $\rho \in \mathbb{B}(H^A \otimes H^B)$ exhibits distillability if and only if there exists a positive integer n along with rank-2 projectors P and Q such that the unnormalized state $\rho' = P \otimes Q \rho^{\otimes n} P \otimes Q$ is entangled, specifically acting on a 2×2 subspace within $H^A \otimes H^B$. Consequently, distillable entanglement can be viewed as a manifestation of two-qubit entanglement. Conversely, entanglement dilution is the reverse process, wherein large copies of perfectly entangled states are transformed into less entangled states through Local Operations and Classical Communication (LOCC) with high fidelity. The objective of the entanglement dilution process is to maximize the inverse ratio of k to n, which defines the distillable entanglement (as described in Kwiat et al. [32]).

4.4 Entanglement cost

Entanglement cost serves as a metric for assessing entanglement, with its primary objective being the quantification of the ebits needed to replicate a state through LOCC operations (as discussed in Wang and Wilde [33]). It's worth noting that this method allows for the concurrent preparation of numerous copies. Consequently, the entanglement cost represents the ebits required per individual copy of the state. It's also noteworthy that the replication process can be approximated, provided that the degree of accuracy can be improved by simultaneously creating multiple copies.

Let P_+ represent a projection operator onto a Bell state denoted as $P_+ := |\Phi^+\rangle \langle \Phi^+|$, with $|\Phi^+\rangle = (|00\rangle + |11\rangle)/\sqrt{2}$. The objective of the entanglement cost is to quantify the achievable rate m/n for converting $P_+^{\otimes m}$ into $\rho^{\otimes n}$ using a LOCC operation denoted as Λ. Given the inherent difficulty of achieving this conversion with absolute precision, we aim to approximate it as $\Lambda(P_+^{\otimes m}) \approx \rho^{\otimes n}$. The quality of this approximation is assessed using a distance metric, such as the Bures distance, trace distance, or an appropriate alternative, denoted as $D(\Lambda(P_+^{\otimes m}), \rho^{\otimes n})$. The entanglement cost, denoted as E_c, is defined as the minimum achievable ratio m/n such that the approximation can be made arbitrarily accurate by selecting suitably large values for m and n. This mathematical formulation is presented in [34]:

$$E_c(\rho) = inf \left\{ E | \forall \varepsilon > 0, \exists m, n, \Lambda, |E - \frac{m}{n}| \leq \delta \ et \ D(\Lambda(P_+^{\otimes m}), \rho^{\otimes n}) \leq \varepsilon \right\}. \quad (24)$$

The entanglement cost has been determined to be equivalent to the regularization of the entanglement of formation, as expressed by the following equation:

$$E_c(\rho) = \lim_{n \to +\infty} \frac{1}{n} E_f(\rho^{\otimes n}) \quad (25)$$

Should the entanglement of formation exhibit additivity, the entanglement cost would coincide with the entanglement of formation.

5. Axiomatic approach

In the preceding section, we examined the quantification of entanglement within the framework of LOCC (Local Operations and Classical Communication) transformations in the asymptotic limit. This approach holds particular interest as it can be fully resolved for pure states, showcasing the reversibility of LOCC entanglement manipulation in this context. Consequently, it imposes a unique ordering on pure entangled states through entanglement entropy. However, when dealing with mixed states and LOCC operations, the situation becomes significantly more complex, and reversibility is no longer guaranteed.

The concurrent loss of a complete ordering of quantum states in terms of LOCC entanglement interconversion rates implies that establishing an entanglement classification solely based on LOCC operations would be exceedingly intricate.

Nevertheless, there is an alternative approach to address this challenge by adopting a more axiomatic perspective. We can define real-valued evaluation functions that adhere to the fundamental properties of entanglement, as discussed earlier, and employ these functions to quantify the degree of entanglement present in a given quantum state. This method forms the basis for defining most entanglement measures. Over the years, various such measures have been proposed, as elaborated upon in the previous section, including entanglement distillation and entanglement cost, among others. While some of these measures have clear physical interpretations, others are purely axiomatic, and we will delve into them in this section.

Within this section, we will expound upon and present a set of fundamental axioms that any entanglement measure should meet. This exploration will enable us to introduce additional quantities beyond the two significant measures already introduced for mixed states ($E_C(\rho)$ and $D(\rho)$). So, what specific properties should a robust entanglement measure exhibit? An entanglement measure is a mathematical concept designed to encapsulate the core characteristics associated with entanglement and ideally should have a connection to practical operational procedures. Depending on your objectives, this may give rise to a range of desirable properties. Below is a compilation of potential postulates for entanglement measures, recognizing that not every proposed measure satisfies all of these criteria.

1. A quantification of entanglement in a bipartite state, denoted as $E(\rho)$, is defined as a mapping from the density matrix to a positive real value

$$\rho \;\rightarrow\; E(\rho) \;\in \mathbb{R}^+ \tag{26}$$

In the case of arbitrary bipartite systems, it is common practice to incorporate a normalization factor to ensure that the maximum entangled state is set to a value of 1.

2. $E(\rho) = 0$ if the state is separable.

3. E does not increase on average under LOCC operations,

$$E(\rho) \geq \sum_i p_i E\left(\frac{A_i \rho A_i^\dagger}{\mathrm{Tr} A_i \rho A_i^\dagger}\right) \tag{27}$$

where the A_i are the Kraus operators describing an LOCC protocol, and the probability of obtaining result i is given by p_i.

4. For a pure state $|\psi\rangle \; \langle\psi|$, the measure reduces to the entanglement entropy

$$E(|\psi\rangle\ \langle\psi|) = (S \otimes \mathrm{Tr}_B)(|\psi\rangle\ \langle\psi|) \tag{28}$$

We will refer to any function denoted as E that fulfills the initial three conditions as a "monotonic entanglement." Meanwhile, the term "entanglement measure" will be employed to describe any quantity that adheres to axioms 1, 2, and 4, while also remaining invariant under deterministic LOCC transformations. It is worth noting that in scholarly literature, these terms are frequently used interchangeably. Furthermore, it is possible to replace Conditions (1)–(4) with an equivalent set of somewhat more abstract conditions, which will be elucidated later. Additionally, some authors commonly impose supplementary criteria for entanglement measures [6, 35]:

- *Convexity* -One frequent instance where an entanglement measure necessitates an extra attribute is the inclusion of the concept of convexity.

$$E\left(\sum_i p_i \rho_i\right) \leq \sum_i p_i E(\rho_i). \tag{29}$$

While it is mathematically convenient, requiring this characteristic can be justified in certain cases as a way to represent the concept of information loss. This concept refers to the transformation from a collection of distinguishable states ρ_i occurring with probabilities p_i to a composite mixture of these states, denoted as $\rho = \sum p_i \rho_i$. Nevertheless, it is important to underscore that specific precautions need to be observed in this context. In the initial scenario, where the states are locally identifiable, the ensemble can be characterized by the quantum state itself.

$$\sum_i p_i |i\rangle_M \langle i| \otimes \rho_i^{AB} \tag{30}$$

Where $|i\rangle_M$ represent an orthonormal basis associated with a particle from one of the two parties. It is evident that when we measure the marker particle M, "it allows us to determine the state of parties A and B". The loss of correlation between i_M and the state ρ_i^{AB} accurately characterizes the process of information erasure, which can be further illustrated by tracing out the marker particle M to yield $\rho = \sum p_i \rho_i$. Since this operation is performed locally, we can stipulate that $E\left(\sum_i p_i |i\rangle_M \langle i| \otimes \rho_i^{AB}\right) \geq E(\rho)$, a requirement that is already implicit in the aforementioned Condition 3. Consequently, there is no strict necessity to introduce convexity, except for the potential mathematical simplicity it may offer.

- *Additivity* - When presented with an entanglement measure denoted as E and a state referred to as σ, we can explore whether the condition $E(\sigma^{\otimes n}) = nE(\sigma)$ holds true for all integer values of n". Such a measure that adheres to this property is termed" additive." Regrettably, some crucial entanglement measure fail to meet this criterion. Therefore, we have refrained from including additivity as a fundamental postulate. Nonetheless, for any measure E" that lacks additivity, a straightforward solution exists to address this limitation. One can introduce a regularized or asymptotic version of the measure.

A more stringent condition to consider could involve requiring total additivity, which implies that for any given pair of states denoted as σ and ρ, the equation

$E(\sigma \otimes \rho) = E(\sigma) + E(\rho)$ must hold. This criterion represents a formidable demand, potentially exceeding the capabilities of quantities that otherwise adhere to the four fundamental properties mentioned earlier. In fact, even basic metrics such as distillation entanglement might not meet this particular requirement. Consequently, we have chosen not to include complete additivity within our set of properties. Nevertheless, it is worth noting that additivity possesses valuable mathematical properties, which we will delve into further within the context of specific measures.

- *Continuity* - The aforementioned Conditions (1)–(3) may appear intuitive. The first two conditions are essentially an extension of the scale definition, and the third condition broadens the concept of entanglement preservation under LOCC operations to encompass probabilistic transformations. On initial inspection, the fourth condition may seem considerably stronger and possibly arbitrary. However, it is revealed that this condition is actually quite reasonable to impose. This is underscored by the fact that $S(\rho_A)$ serves as the reversible conversion rate between pure states in the asymptotic regime, strongly suggesting its appropriateness as the entanglement measure for pure states. This conclusion is further supported by the following noteworthy observation: Any entanglement measure that satisfies the criteria of being both (a) additive on pure states and (b) "sufficiently continuous" must coincide with $S(\rho_A)$ for all pure states.

Prior to delving into the concept of "sufficiently continuous," we will first outline a preliminary argument in support of this assertion. The asymptotic distillation protocol for pure states reveals that from n copies of a pure state denoted as $|\phi\rangle$, it is possible to derive a state ρ_n. This derived state closely approximates the state $|\psi\rangle^{-\otimes nE(|\phi\rangle)}$ within a margin of error ε, where $E(|\phi\rangle)$ signifies the entanglement entropy associated with $|\phi\rangle$. Now, let us consider the scenario where we possess a monotonically increasing entanglement measure L, which exhibits additivity with respect to pure states. In such a case, we can express this relationship as follows:

$$nL(|\phi\rangle) = L\left(|\phi\rangle^{\otimes n}\right) \geq L(\rho_n) \tag{31}$$

where the inequality is due to Condition 3 for entanglement monotones.

5.1 Entanglement witness

Let us denote by M_d the space of $d \times d$ matrices (identified with the space of linear maps from $\mathbb{C}^d$ to $\mathbb{C}^d$), and by PSD_d the cone of positive semidefinite Hermitian (PSD) matrices. We say that a linear application $\Phi : M_d \to M_d$ is positive and verify $\Phi(PSD_d) \subset PSD_d$, and $\Phi : M_d \to M_d$ is completely positive if, for all $n \in \mathbb{N}^*$, the map $\Phi \otimes Id_{M_n}$ is positive. Let $\Phi : M_d \to M_d$ a positive map and $\rho \in D\left(\mathbb{C}^d \otimes \mathbb{C}^d\right)$ a state. It is easy to see that when ρ is separable, the operator $(\Phi \otimes Id)(\rho)$ is positive. By contraposition, as soon as $(\Phi \otimes Id)(\rho)$ has a strictly negative eigenvalue, we can deduce that ρ is entangled. In this case, we say that Φ is an entanglement witness for ρ. The following result holds, which follows from an application of the Hahn-Banach theorem.

Theorem: (Horodecki criterion, [36]). Let ρ be a state on $\mathbb{C}^d \otimes \mathbb{C}^d$. We have the equivalence:

- ρ is entangled
- there exists an entanglement witness for ρ.

An entanglement witness is necessarily a positive but not completely positive map. An example of such a map is the transpose $T : M_d \to M_d$. Remarkably, in dimension 2, the transpose is essentially the unique entanglement witness. This is the content of the following result due to Størmer.

Theorem: (Størmer). Let $\Phi : M_2 \to M_2$ be a positive map. Then there exist two completely positive maps Φ_1 and Φ_2 such that $\Phi = \Phi_1 + \Phi_2 \circ T$.

5.1.1 Positive partial transposition, PPT

The partial transposition of a state $\rho \in D\left(\mathbb{C}^{d_1} \otimes \mathbb{C}^{d_1}\right)$ is defined as $\rho^\Gamma := (T \otimes Id)(\rho)$, and we say that ρ is positive under positive partial transposition (PPT) if the operator ρ^Γ is positive. Any state that is not PPT is entangled. A consequence of the last two specific theorems in dimension 2 is a converse: **Corollary**: A state on $\mathbb{C}^2 \otimes \mathbb{C}^2$ is separable if and only if it is PPT [37, 38].

5.2 Concurrence and negativity

A function that fulfills the aforementioned criteria is referred to as a monotonic entanglement measure. While it is possible to impose further conditions, like convexity and additivity, these constraints may be relaxed, as they are not met by certain entanglement measures. An illustration of an entanglement measure applicable to pure states can be found in Wootters' concurrence, which is defined by the following Eq. [39]:

$$C(\rho) = \sqrt{2\left(1 - Tr\left[\rho^{(A)^2}\right]\right)}. \tag{32}$$

Moreover, the previously mentioned approach can be expanded to encompass mixed states by computing the convex roof of the concurrence for such states. In the context of a 2×2 scenario, the concurrence assumes a straightforward expression:

$$C(\rho) = max\,(0, \lambda_1 - \lambda_2 - \lambda_3 - \lambda_4) \tag{33}$$

where the $\lambda_{i}{}_{i=1}^{4}$ are the eigenvalues of:

$$M = \sqrt{\sqrt{\rho}\tilde{\rho}\sqrt{\rho}} \;\; : \;\; \tilde{\rho} = \sigma_y \otimes \sigma_y \rho^* \sigma_y \otimes \sigma_y \tag{34}$$

Ultimately, an uncomplicated measure of entanglement that lends itself to straightforward computation for mixed states is negativity, as discussed in Ref. [40]. This measure is associated with the breach of the PPT criterion and is connected through the following relationship:

$$N(\rho) = \frac{\left\|\rho^{T_B}\right\|_1 - 1}{2} \tag{35}$$

Another measure is the logarithmic negativity [41]:

$$E_N(\rho) = log_2 \|\rho^{T_B}\|_1 \tag{36}$$

- can be zero, even if the state is entangled (if the state is PPT entangled).
- does not reduce to the entanglement entropy for pure states like most other entanglement measures.
- is additive over tensor products $E_N(\rho \otimes \sigma) = E_N(\rho) + E_N(\sigma)$

In summary, this chapter's exploration into quantifying entanglement has yielded a comprehensive comprehension of the fundamental properties and operational aspects of this intriguing quantum phenomenon. Beginning with an examination of basic characteristics and quantum operations, we have delved into the essence of entanglement itself, emphasizing its non-classical foundation, which underlies the principles of quantum mechanics. We have also scrutinized the local manipulation of entangled quantum states from an operational perspective, shedding light on the complexities involved in manipulating these states while preserving their fragile entanglement.

Furthermore, our discussion has extended to the manipulation of bipartite states, where we introduced concepts like entanglement of formation, entanglement distillation, and entanglement cost. These notions have underscored the versatile nature of entanglement in various quantum protocols and applications, highlighting its profound significance in the realm of quantum information theory.

Additionally, we explored an axiomatic approach to quantifying entanglement, introducing the concept of an entanglement witness and measures like concurrence and negativity. These approaches offer valuable tools for evaluating and quantifying entanglement in diverse quantum systems, enabling us to grasp the extent of entanglement's impact in various scenarios.

In conclusion, it is evident that quantifying entanglement transcends mere theoretical pursuit; it has become a practical necessity in advancing quantum technologies and information processing. The interconnected nature of quantum states and their entanglement opens up new possibilities in fields such as quantum computing, cryptography, and communication.

A. Appendix

A.1 Pauli operator

X bit-flip

$$\sigma_x = \begin{pmatrix} 0 & 1 \\ 1 & 0 \end{pmatrix} \tag{37}$$

Y bit et phase-flip.
The operation Y is defined as:

$$\sigma_y = \begin{pmatrix} 0 & -i \\ i & 0 \end{pmatrix} \tag{38}$$

Z phase-flip.
The operation Z is defined as:

$$\sigma_z = \begin{pmatrix} 1 & 0 \\ 0 & -1 \end{pmatrix} \tag{39}$$

A.2 Standard rotations

Standard rotation gates are those that define rotations around the Pauli $P = X, Y, Z$ axes. They are defined as follows:

Rotation around the X-axis

$$R_x(\theta) = \begin{pmatrix} \cos(\theta/2) & -i\sin\theta/2 \\ -i\sin\theta/2 & \cos\theta/2 \end{pmatrix} \tag{40}$$

Rotation around the Y-axis

$$R_y(\theta) = \begin{pmatrix} \cos(\theta/2) & -\sin\theta/2 \\ \sin\theta/2 & \cos\theta/2 \end{pmatrix} \tag{41}$$

Rotation around the Z-axis

$$R_z(\theta) = \begin{pmatrix} e^{-i\phi/2} & 0 \\ 0 & e^{i\phi/2} \end{pmatrix} \tag{42}$$

A.3 Definition

Ebit: An ebit is a unit of bipartite entanglement, the amount of entanglement contained in a perfectly entangled state of two qubits (Bell state). If a state is said to have X ebits of entanglement (quantified by an entanglement measure), it has the same amount of entanglement (in that measure) as X Bell states. If a task requires Y ebits, it can be accomplished with Y or more Bell states, but not with fewer.

Ebit: An ebit is a unit of bipartite entanglement, representing the amount of entanglement contained in a perfectly entangled two-qubit state (Bell state). If a state is said to have X ebits of entanglement (quantified by an entanglement measure), it has the same amount of entanglement (in that measure) as X Bell states. If a task requires Y ebits, it can be accomplished with Y or more Bell states, but not with fewer.

Author details

Bilal Benzimoun[1*] and Abdelali Sajia[2]

1 Department of Physics, Clark University, Worcester, Massachusetts, USA

2 Department of Physics, and Center for Quantum Science and Engineering, Stevens Institute of Technology, Hoboken, New Jersey, USA

*Address all correspondence to: b.benzimoun@gmail.com

References

[1] Bell JS. Speakable and Unspeakable in Quantum Mechanics. Cambridge: Cambridge University Press; 1987

[2] Yin J, Cao Y, Yong H-L, Ren J-G, Liang H, Liao S-K, et al. Bounding the speed of'spooky action at a distance. Physical Review Letters. 2013;**110**(26): 260407

[3] Bokulich A, Jaeger G. Philosophy of Quantum Information and Entanglement. Cambridge, UK: Cambridge University Press; 2010

[4] Kocher CA. Time correlations in the detection of successively emitted photons. Annals of Physics. 1971;**65**(1): 1-18

[5] Dirac P. Note on exchange phenomena in the Thomas atom. Mathematical Proceedings of the Cambridge Philosophical Society. 2008; **26**(3):376

[6] Horodecki R, Horodecki P, Horodecki M, Horodecki K. Quantum entanglement. Reviews of Modern Physics. 2009;**81**(2):865-942

[7] Christenson N, Kauffmann HF, Pullerits T, Mancal T. Origin of long-lived coherences in light-harvesting complexes. The Journal of Physical Chemistry. B. 2012;**116**(25):7449-7454

[8] Nielsen MA. Conditions for a class of entanglement transformations. Physical Review Letters. 1999;**83**:436-439

[9] Jonathan D, Plenio MB. Entanglement-assisted local manipulation of pure quantum states. Physical Review Letters. 1999;**83**:3566

[10] Hurley W, Sudarshan G. Algebraic study of a class of relativistic wave equations. Annals of Physics. 1974;**85**: 546-590

[11] Mark WM. Quantum Information Theory. Vol. arXiv:1106. Cambridge, UK: Cambridge University Press; 2017. p. 1445

[12] Benzimoun B, Daoud M. Geometrical analysis and entanglement measure of symmetric multiqubit states. International Journal of Geometric Methods in Modern Physics. 2020; **17**(08):2050119

[13] Albrecht R. Computer Algebra: Symbolic and Algebraic Computation. Vol. 4. Berlin, Germany: Springer Science and Business Media; 2012

[14] Masanes L, Liang YC, Doherty AC. All bipartite entangled states display some hidden nonlocality. Physical Review Letters. 2007;**100**(090403):7-9

[15] De Closets F. Ne dites pas à Dieu ce qu'il doit faire. Media Diffusion, coll. Montrouge, France: "social Science"; 2014. p. 448

[16] Boyd R. Nonlinear Optics. 3rd ed. Cambridge, MA, USA: Academic Press; 2008. pp. 13-15

[17] Kocher CA, Commins E. Polarization correlation of photons emitted in an atomic Cascade. Physical Review Letters. 1967;**18**(15):575-577

[18] Meekhof DM, Monroe C, King BE, Itano WM, Wineland DJ. Generation of nonclassical motional states of a trapped atom. Physical Review Letters. 1996;**76**: 1796; Erratum Phys. Rev. Lett. 77, 2346, (1996)

[19] Raymond et al. The Rac GTPase-activating protein RotundRacGAP

interferes with Drac1 and Dcdc42 signaling in Drosophila melanogaster. The Journal of Biological Chemistry. 2001;**276**(38):35909-35916

[20] Hald A. Weed vegetation (wild flora) of long established organic versus conventional cereal fields in Denmark. Annals of Applied Biology. 2008;**134**(3): 307-314. DOI: 10.1111/j.1744-7348.1999. tb05269.x

[21] Julsgaard B, Kozhekin A, Polzik ES. Experimental long-lived entanglement of two macroscopic objects. Nature. 2001;**413**:400-403

[22] Emery G et al. Asymmetric Rab 11 endosomes regulate delta recycling and specify cell fate in the drosophila nervous system. Cell. 2005;**122**(5):763-773

[23] Chen YH et al. Observed relationships between Arctic longwave cloud forcing and cloud parameters using a neural network. Journal of Climate. 2006;**19**:4087-4104. DOI: 10.1175/JCLI3839.1

[24] Muschik C, Muschik CA, Hammerer K, Polzik ES, Cirac JI. Efficient quantum memory and entanglement between light and an atomic ensemble using magnetic fields. Physical Review A. 2006;**73**(6):062329

[25] Chitambar E et al. Everything you always wanted to know about LOCC (but were afraid to ask). Communications in Mathematical Physics. 2012;**328**:303. arXiv:1210.4583

[26] Gour G, Wallach NR. Classification of multipartite entanglement of all finite dimensionality. Physical Review Letters. 2013;**111**:060502

[27] Vidal G. Entanglement monotones. Journal of Modern Optics. 2000;**47**:355

[28] Sudarshan ECG, Mathews PM, et al. Stochastic dynamics of quantum-mechanical systems. Physical Review. American Physical Society (APS). 1961; **121**(3):920-924

[29] Eisert J, Cramer M, Plenio MB. Colloquium: Area laws for the entanglement entropy. Reviews of Modern Physics. 2010;**82**(1):277-306

[30] Bennett CH et al. Concentrating partial entanglement by local operations. Physical Review A. 1996;**53**(4):2046-2052

[31] Bennett CH, Wooters WK. Purification of Noisy entanglement and faithful teleportation via Noisy channels. Physical Review Letters. 1996;**76**(5): 722-725

[32] Kwiat PG et al. Experimental entanglement distillation and 'hidden' non-locality. Nature. 2001;**409**(6823): 1014-1017

[33] Wang X, Wilde MM. Physical Review Letters. 2020;**125**:040502

[34] Hayden PM, Horodecki M, Terhal BM. The asymptotic entanglement cost of preparing a quantum state. Journal of Physics A: Mathematical and General. 2001;**34**(35): 6891-6898

[35] Eric C, Gilad G. Quantum resource theories. Reviews of Modern Physics. 2019;**91**(2):025001

[36] Horodecki M, Horodecki P, et al. Physics Letters A. 1996;**223**:1

[37] Peres A. Physical Review Letters. 1996;**77**:1413

[38] Benzimoun B, Daoud M. On a biseparability criterion of bipartite qudit state. Chinese Physics B. 2019;**28**(08): 080302

[39] Wootters WK. Entanglement of formation of an arbitrary state of two qubits. Physical Review Letters. 1998;**80**: 2245

[40] Zyczkowski K, Horodecki P, Sanpera A, Lewenstein M. Volume of the set of separable states. Physical Review A. 1998;**58**:883-892

[41] Plenio MB. The logarithmic negativity: A full entanglement monotone that is not convex. Physical Review Letters. 2005;**95**:090503

Chapter 4

Mechanizing Quantum Error Correction through Entangled Quantum Machine Learning Techniques

Theresa Melvin

Abstract

Noisy intermediate scale quantum (NISQ) systems are susceptible to errors that culminate in near-one hundred percent data loss. This is due to quantum state fragility and the incredibly high quantum communication error rates caused by decoherence, or quantum noise. As such, stabilizing qubit operational imprecision in quantum information processing is a critical area of research in quantum computing. Adaptive quantum machine learning (QML) methods, like unsupervised and fully entangled quantum generative adversarial networks is one such technology theorized to provide a breakthrough in quantum error suppression. Mechanizing the quantum error detection and correction process with QML provides a path forward from today's monolithic quantum computers running almost exclusively single-core quantum processing unit (QPU) designs, to the next generation of federated quantum computers using multi-core QPUs. Automating the detection and correction of quantum errors in powerful NISQ devices will pave the way for fault-tolerant quantum computing, making quantum speeds at quantum scale suddenly achievable.

Keywords: quantum machine learning (QML), quantum generative adversarial network (QGAN), quantum error correction (QEC), quantum communication error rate (QCER), quantum error correcting code (QECC), noisy intermediate scale quantum (NISQ)

1. Introduction

The mere mention of *quantum speeds at quantum scale* when referencing today's noisy intermediate scale quantum (NISQ) devices, which are susceptible to environmental errors so severe that they result in near-one hundred percent data loss will grind a room full of quantum researchers to a steadfast halt. Google's AI Quantum team found this out when they asserted "Quantum Supremacy" [1] in 2019, basing their Sycamore fidelity results on 1% signal in 99% noise. Google's work, however, provided the quantum research community with valuable insight. Most notably, it forced quantum developers to stop and ask: what is it going to take to achieve a

IntechOpen

quantum computer that is not only as reliable and as scalable as an ordinary classical computer, but as fast as a quantum computer?

This chapter explores quantum computing technology, the errors that inhibit this technology, and the adaptive quantum machine learning (QML) methods developed as an answer to stabilize this qubit operational imprecision. Special attention is paid to unsupervised and fully entangled quantum generative adversarial networks, and how they have emerged over the past 5 years to become an important QML technology in quantum error correction.

This chapter is organized as follows: section two begins with an overview of the quantum information process, followed by section three's quantum errors on NISQ devices. Section four focuses on quantum error correction research, a necessary background for section five's quantum machine learning discussion. This then leads to the unsupervised quantum generative adversarial network noise (uQGAN) model experiment in section six, followed by chapter summary in section seven's conclusion.

2. Quantum information processing

Quantum bits or qubits are fragile and packaged with quantum information (QI). Prior to transmitting this QI through a qubit communication channel, the QI is encoded. Next, quantum error detection and correction (QED/C) methods, like stabilizer codes, continuously measure the quantum waves, called syndromes [2]. While the quantum states are not directly measured since that would cause the amplitudinal wave to collapse into a particle [3], the parity of qubits is automatically adjusted based on measurements to correct the quantum state [4]. The QI is then decoded, and the transmission is complete. Thus, stabilizer code performs a rudimentary form of QED/C which successfully suppresses quantum errors (QE/s) during quantum information processing (QIP) execution against trivial programs. This solution, however, lacks scale due to the high number of physical qubits [5] required to encode a single logical qubit.

Presently, the qubit communications channel used in QIP consists of a hard-wired and direct integration into a single-core quantum processing unit (QPU) [6]. Due to its convoluted integrated network design, this single-core QPU design is rife with challenges and requires manual intervention for quantum interactions [7]. This configuration generates noise, vibrations, and temperature fluctuations that generate errors, faults, and decoherence [8] causing irreparable damage to the QIP operation, stifling QC performance.

A quantum communication error rate (QCER) benchmark is used to observe the QIP operation, and it measures the probability that something went wrong with the qubit during the quantum gate operation (I.e., quantum error rate) against how accurately the actual output matches the desired output (I.e., quantum state fidelity). Unlike classical calculations, which are deterministic (predictable) and produce expected results and outcomes, QC computations are non-deterministic (random) and therefore do not possess any specific outcome. As such, QCERs are exceptionally high during QIP due to the inherently brittle state of qubits, illustrating the stark immaturity of modern QC technology. To advance quantum computing to practical use, efficient QED/C methods are needed for common QEs to reduce QCERs and safely teleport QI during the QIP.

3. Superconducting NISQ device errors

This section explores the types of quantum errors observed in superconducting phase qubits, one of the most popular quantum computing technologies in use. Errors represent an organic part of any computer operation. However, QC errors are considerably more complex than classical errors. Disturbances that cause QC errors occur when quantum states are not prepared properly, they exceed their target, or they drift away [9]. For this reason, the QEs are often distinct to the underlying QC hardware, and any associated error detection and correction methods would therefore need to be equally subjective.

3.1 Qubit-based QC technologies

The largest QCs currently in use are gate-based quantum computers, also known as near-term QCs, or noisy intermediate-scale quantum (NISQ) devices [10, 11]. These systems are built with superconducting qubits, trapped ions, spin qubits, semiconductors, photonics, nitrogen-vacancy center (NVC), nuclear magnetic resonance (NMR), and quantum dots [4, 12, 13], to name a few.

Current NISQ systems possess anywhere from dozens of qubits to 40 qubits like one core of Rigetti's dual-core QPU [14, 15], to 54 qubits, like Google's Sycamore [16], to 433 qubits, like IBM's Osprey, the largest QC in existence [17] as of the time of this writing. Yet, even with 80 qubit dual-core QPUs [15] and 4000 qubit QC systems planned [17] it should be noted that NISQ devices will still not be advanced enough to achieve fault tolerance without a significant reduction in QEs. This will preclude the level of scale needed for quantum supremacy [1], where problems that elude classical computers are consistently solved in a timely manner. Likewise, with near-total data loss, it remains equally challenging to achieve any kind of quantum advantage [18] in a commercial setting until the QE issue is suitably addressed.

3.2 Quantum error correction for NISQ devices

The focus of this chapter is leveraging QML for QEC in superconducting phase qubits, one of the most popular NISQ QC technologies in use today. The three primary methods used to address QEs on this type of NISQ device are, error:

- Suppression
- Mitigation
- Correction

This chapter focuses exclusively on the third type of QE: quantum error correction (QEC) since it is closely associated with the field of QML. Quantum machine learning intersects the fields of quantum computing with ML. For this reason, QML is posited as one possible method of detecting quantum errors as they occur and then summarily correcting them in real-time. The challenge with putting this theory into practice is the stark number of NISQ QEs and the immense complexity behind all these errors. A glimpse into the difficulty of this developmental task is highlighted below.

3.2.1 Common causes of decoherence on NISQ devices

Quantum processors on NISQ devices generate noise, vibrations, and temperature fluctuations [7, 18]. This in turn creates errors, faults, and other types of communications failures, leading to exorbitantly high QCERs, which stifles QC performance [19]. As a result, very few non-trivial quantum programs are executed to completion. Moreover, non-trivial programs that are executed to completion rarely obtain the correct results. This is due to environmental noise, also called decoherence, which creates an assortment of QEs that interfere with the NISQ device. A few of the most common errors are discussed in turn below.

The three most common types of quantum errors are bit-flip errors (bfe/s), phase-flip errors (pfe/s), or a combination of the two, known as bit-and-phase-flip errors (bpfe/s). While both classical and quantum computers contend with bfes [4] which modify the original binary state from a zero to a one or a one to a zero, QCs must also contend with pfes, which modify the quantum state, changing the qubit from a positive to a negative, (or vice-versa). Phase-flip errors in turn represent the most prevalent type of QC error, and as such most QED/C research focuses on pfe prevention [20]. However, the third and most difficult type of quantum error to detect and correct is the combined bpfe, in which both the original and quantum states are altered during QIP [3]. While combination errors are rare, they represent one of the most difficult QED/C problems to solve.

In addition to the above QEs, many other errors impact QCs. These include, but are not limited to gates, mixed unitary, phase damping, amplitude damping, depolarization, asymmetric depolarization, and resets [2, 20]. This extended error list stems from QM, with properties like superposition that allow the quantum state to be many different states simultaneously. The relative phase and amplitude of the superimposed states ultimately determines the properties of the entire quantum state. These QC devices can generate error in many ways, for many different reasons, with different Gates (Hadamard, Pauli, R, etc.) all providing their own individual errors.

Next, according to [7] phase damping errors occur when the coherence of the quantum state is destroyed due to the relative phases of the superposed states randomly changing with time. In turn, amplitude damping errors occur when the quantum state changes due to environmental energy dissipation. Depolarization errors, or the sudden death of maximally entangled qubits [21] results in the loss of QI. Furthermore, this noisy channel can be either one-sided (symmetric) or multi-sided (asymmetric) [8]. For these types of NISQ specific device errors, the classical error correction techniques are ineffective at correcting quantum errors.

4. Quantum error correction research

Quantum error detection and correction techniques are required to protect qubits from decoherence and noise during QIP, facilitating the successful teleportation of QI [3, 13]. Unfortunately, many obstacles exist to making QCs error-resistant or fault-tolerant. First, the no-cloning theorem [22] in QM prohibits an unknown quantum state from being reliably copied without destroying the original quantum state. Therefore, duplicating an arbitrary unknown quantum state is forbidden, meaning quantum data cannot be copied and pasted between qubits the way classical data is replicated using classical bits. Next, the Heisenberg uncertainty principle dictates that unknown quantum states cannot be fully measured without inducing a QE and destroying the state [2, 20, 23]. As such, unlike a classical experiment, it is impossible to observe a quantum experiment without destroying the experiment.

Quantum error correction is a research area addressing real-time quantum state feedback and in-sequence measurements necessary for QED/C. While there are many different types of error correction for classical systems, the most common fault-tolerant approaches are checkpointing, parity checks, error correction code (ECC), and redundancy [4, 5, 8, 18, 20]. Checkpointing cannot be used on QCs for either QED or QEC due to the no-cloning theorem. In turn, parity checks require an extra (parity) bit to be attached to the data for redundancy. A count of each data's parity bit confirms if the data was successfully transmitted. Parity checks do work for detecting errors on QC; however, parity checks do not offer a method for correcting quantum errors. To determine the parity count of the QI requires a measurement. This violates Heisenberg's uncertainty principle, which asserts that an unknown quantum state cannot be measured without destroying the state.

Next, ECC encodes the entire byte stream comprising the data transmission into a single word. ECC does work for QCs, but only for bit flips, where the qubit changes from a 0 to a 1 (and vice-versa). ECC uses a majority voting system, flipping the corrupt (non-matching) bit to match the other (matching) bits. ECC, however, does not work for quantum phase errors, where the qubit changes from a positive to a negative (and vice-versa), since phase errors do not exist in classical systems.

The final classical error correction technique discussed is redundancy. Redundancy simply sends the same data repeatedly to ensure transmission success. While this method does work for QC at a small scale, satisfying both QED and QEC, redundancy is impractical due to the massive number of physical qubits required to support the repeatability of QI transmissions. To achieve quantum scale would require several orders of magnitude more physical qubits due to interactions among nonadjacent qubits operating on and correcting redundant encoded quantum data. This level of massive redundancy is cost-prohibitive for QCs.

4.1 Stabilizer codes

Stabilizer codes are a quantum error correction encoding process affording QI redundancy for a single physical qubit. The stabilizer code wraps the physical qubit containing the QI with multiple logical qubits. Using stabilizer code, the state of a single physical qubit is encoded with several ancilla or helper qubits, creating a single stabilizer code for quantum error correcting code (QECC). The number of ancilla is determined by the stabilizer code used, with four, seven, and nine qubit models common, depending on the model selected and the type of quantum error to be corrected. For instance, the five-qubit stabilizer code is the smallest model capable of correcting either bit-flip or phase-flip errors, but only for a single quantum error. This is distinguished from Shor's original nine-qubit code, which corrected for two-qubit errors.

4.2 Surface codes

Topological codes, such as surface codes, overcome the quantum-scale challenges of stabilizer codes. Surface codes leverage a two-dimensional lattice of qubits with nearest-neighbor coupling, affording integrated QECC. Due to the integrated qubit design, surface codes scale well, revealing a high tolerance for locally correctable quantum errors. However, surface codes are in their infancy and are expensive to produce. This renders the technology largely out of reach for the mainstream quantum research community.

4.3 Quantum machine learning models

Neural decoding algorithms and generative adversarial networks (GAN/s) are two types of ML models with demonstrated, albeit small-scale, QECC success [11, 13, 24]. The QML models are trained on quantum error-injected data, the quantum algorithms eventually learn the probability distribution of the QEs and correct the error chains to recover the correct quantum states. In theory, this is one way to produce a fault tolerant NISQ system. This is the underlying premise of the section that follows.

5. Quantum machine learning

Traditional ML merged mathematical algorithms with statistical modeling, providing a method for computers to learn complex tasks with minimal instruction. Quantum machine learning is an emerging theoretical field combining quantum algorithms with traditional ML. Just as ML techniques are used on classical computers for big data processing, QML is envisaged to leverage qubits and multi-core QPUs to support the computational needs of next generation full-stack quantum computing workloads. However, QML's necessary quantum algorithm (QALGO) innovation has remained slow to advance due to the lack of realistic QC technology and decoherence struggles. These limitations impede QML execution, performance, and evaluation of complex real-world algorithms.

With advancements in QML and QC research on the rise, practical quantum uses for industry are starting to emerge, prompting further investment in the field. As more companies discover quantum applications capable of revenue generation, quantum will eventually be adopted into mainstream industry. This increased QC demand for commercial access will drive further QC innovation, rapidly advancing QALGO development and moving QCs closer to achieving a total quantum advantage over all classical systems.

5.1 Quantum algorithms

Quantum algorithm development has been an active area of research since 1994, when Shor's Algorithm exponentially sped up integer factor detection for a large number [25]. With quantum computing still in its infancy, hundreds of QALGOs exist today for many different use cases. As such, anything a classical computer can do today, a QC can also do [26]. Likewise, provable quantum advantage is known for a few dozen QALGOs [18] though innovation remains slow to advance due to the lack of realistic QCs, which impedes real-world QALGO performance and evaluation. While quantum developers work to bridge this QC hardware gap using classical computers, classical bits lack the quantum mechanical properties of quantum bits, which renders their hybrid quantum-classical algorithm (HALGO) work deficient and marginally irrelevant to QALGO development.

Unlike HALGOs, QALGOs completely rely on unnatural quantum physics principles, which are counterintuitive to classical physics. The QALGO's non-intuitive and strange behavior facilitates quantum's massive scale [18, 27, 28]. In turn, HALGOs remain computationally limited by their classical computing, which is constrained by the laws of contemporary physics. For instance, QC-generated probability distributions are hard for classical computers to sample since comparable quantum mechanical conditions do not exist in a classical computer system.

Next, probability distributions for a classical ML problem possess either a positive or negative. In turn, QML probability distributions leverage the QM property of superposition, allowing QALGO results to be positive, negative, or a combination of the two (superposed). HALGOs must approximate the quantum probability distribution since the classical hardware is physically incapable of simulating a large number of quantum wave excitations [29]. This is problematic since the accuracy of these estimates remains largely unknown and borders on conjecture. While QALGO development remains challenged by the lack of mature QC hardware capabilities, QALGO studies continually produce innovative potential. One such area of QALGO advancement is recent quantum generative adversarial network (QGAN) research.

5.2 Quantum generative adversarial networks

A generative adversarial network (GAN) is a type of semi-supervised or unsupervised neural network used for creating high-quality synthetic data. Derived from a novel zero-sum game concept, a single GAN framework is comprised of two independent neural networks, called a generator (G) and discriminator (D). Each GAN neural network (the G and the D) then attempts to outperform the other, forcing each neutral network to continually retrain. This process repeats until the GAN model achieves no further performance gain.

Generative adversarial network technology has matured considerably over the past decade, with GANs now successfully modeling molecular synthesis [30] and dark matter [31]. They are further used to: detect and assess cyber-risk [32], identify counterfeiting and fraud [33], accelerate financial time-series modeling [34], and explore human-centered computing [27]. Likewise, GAN technology has shown success with photorealistic image creation and enhancement [35], video prediction [27], and audio processing [22]. GAN application has even successfully branched into natural language processing (NLP) and natural language understanding (NLU) [21], where it summarizes text and generates semantics. While GANs have become a prolific data creation [36] tool in AI, their application remains limited due to both GAN complexity and classical system performance limitations.

Challenges surrounding GANs include vanishing gradients, mode collapse, and failures to converge or reach a Nash Equilibrium [28, 31, 37]. Vanishing gradients are common when the G fails to train due to an ineffective D [31, 38]. When a G lacks heterogeneity among its generated samples and supplies the D with only a single sample category (mode), either a partial or complete mode collapse occurs. The difference between partial and complete mode collapse is that some (partial) or all (complete) of the G's generated samples are mapped to identical D-output. Lastly, GANs routinely fail to converge, oscillating from one sample generation to the next without achieving any type of equilibrium.

To date, most QGAN research has been HALGO rather than QALGO-focused [31, 38]. Because HALGOs are leveraged, a hybrid quantum-classical GAN (HGAN) is created. These HGANs are neither entirely classical nor entirely quantum since a portion of the GAN process is executed on a classical computer. At the same time, the remainder of the GAN execution occurs on a QC. As a result, many of the same challenges that plague a classical GAN (CGAN) also encumber HGANs. Moreover, as discussed below, HGANs have the additional and arduous QML challenge of encoding classical data into a quantum state.

For these reasons, the goal has been a true quantum GAN, with both the G and D running on a parameterized or variational quantum circuit (VQC). Recent QLAGO research on entangled QGAN models has been groundbreaking [31, 38], successfully circumventing common GAN errors. Based on recent QGAN innovations, a QML-mechanized solution for QED/C, placing equal emphasis on QALGO and NISQ hardware, seems plausible.

5.2.1 Hybrid-QGAN

Until 2019, quantum-GAN research leveraged quantum-classical hybrid algorithms for GAN frameworks almost exclusively [22, 27, 37, 39–41]. While this work was often referred to as a quantum-GAN, these were HGANs. A typical HGAN design leveraged a VQC for the G, while the D utilized a classical neural network, thereby avoiding the quantum random access memory (QRAM) input bottleneck associated with encoding the real classical data into a quantum state.

The VQC's connection topology, where qubits were directly connected to the QPU, contributed to HGAN success since variables could be added or tuned, for both the D and G during training [37, 39–41]. Other HGAN research leveraged binary encoding [41] and amplitude encoding [39] for classical-quantum data preparation, which required considerable resources for the QML computation. A final QC-inspired unitary transformation learning approach [41] attempted classical-quantum data loads using fewer resources.

The VQC flexibility for G-tuning helped to ensure HGAN convergence to a Nash equilibrium. The QC further helped to overcome many of the CGAN training stability challenges [22, 39]. Likewise, HGAN performance times were typically lower than an equivalent CGAN model [22, 27, 40] pushing GAN technology closer to real-world performance expectations. Still, the HGAN's decreased performance from encoding classical data into a quantum state nullified all QC gains realized [31, 38, 42], thereby requiring exploration into true fully entangled QC GANs.

5.2.2 Fully-entangled QGAN

To extend GAN application fully to QCs, a new QGAN architecture was introduced [31, 38, 42] where both the input and output were comprised entirely of quantum data. This new QGAN design forced all GAN operations onto the QC, bypassing the classical system entirely. As a result, the QML and QRAM performance encumbrances encountered by previous HGANs were eradicated. Unfortunately, bypassing classical systems and forgoing classical-quantum data encoding severely limited QGAN use case applicability since current quantum datasets are infinitesimally small.

This was first illustrated by [42] in their trivial but important QGAN experiment where, using a superconducting transmon qubit, both real and fake data was stored in bosonic modes using an alternating algorithm. Real quantum data was created in an arbitrary state using the bosonic microwave mode, which maintained control of the transmon qubit and the bosonic mode. The QGEN next created the transmon's fake data from the real quantum state. The QDIS then measured the axis angles of the transmon qubit to determine the ground state. From this point, the traditional GAN adversarial game was played, with gradient measurements calculated to maximize the discriminator for the QDIS' turn or maximizing the generator for the QGEN's turn.

The adversarial learning process was repeated until either a preset limit was reached or the optimized QDIS discriminator was smaller than a preset threshold. Fidelities as high as 99.1% were achieved for both the real and fake data quantum states. This experiment revealed that a QGAN could achieve convergence without knowing whether the QGEN's data was real or fake or the QDIS' selected axis measurement.

A second equally important piece of QGAN research to emerge was [38], who addressed classical-quantum data load limitation issues while building off [42] in their efforts to mitigate HGAN mode collapse issues and convergence errors. Using Google Sycamore, [38] created a novel entangled QGAN that entangled both real and fake QGEN data at the QDIS. This was a deviation from previous QGAN work, which provided the QDIS with either real or fake data, but not both. Moreover, in previous HGAN work, the QGEN supplied a classical discriminator (D) with either the real or the fake sample. Thus, it was impossible to entangle HGAN-QDIS data, an incongruity that routinely caused non-convergence and oscillations due to mode collapse.

This two-qubit entangled QGAN from [38] overcame the mode collapse issues that plagued previous HGAN research and their QGAN converged to a Nash equilibrium. They further showed their QDIS effective at recognizing and suppressing certain quantum errors on Google NISQ devices. While more work was required to determine the feasibility of unsupervised QED/C, [38] showed promise since gradient calculations on QML models are time-consuming, leaving NISQ devices prone to QEs. Lastly, and perhaps most relevant to quantum application development, they demonstrated that their entangled QGAN could create an approximate QRAM for loading classical data in superposition, thereby expediting the classical-quantum data encoding process.

The work of [38] was furthered by [31] who performed three tests of varying hardware and software complexity, against the new entangled QGAN developed by [38]. Google's Cirq open-source quantum python framework was used by [31] to prepare the VQCs for their experiments, while TensorFlow Quantum (TFQ) was used to add the physical circuits as model layers. Two, four, and six-qubit models were trained using TensorFlow with an Adam optimizer set to a 0.01 learning rate. Noise was then artificially injected into gate rotation angles by adding a gate with a random error after each CNOT, iSWAP, or CZ gate.

The first experiment by [31] consisted of a single layer of randomly selected predefined rotation angles where a simulation performed both a perfect swap test and an adversarial swap test. Their experiments leveraged only the QGEN and thus did not require entangled QGAN training. Results showed the perfect swap test generally performed better. Moreover, the entangled QGAN's mode was elevated, indicating the data was highly dispersed, a problem notorious to traditional CGANs, since GANs, in general, are difficult to train. Notably, dissimilar rotation angles revealed that while the two amplitudes were identical, the two quantum states were, in fact, different.

The second experiment by [31] challenged the entangled QGAN further, increasing the qubit count and QGEN layers and using real Hamiltonian data produced by a variational quantum eigensolver (VQE). The goal was for the entangled QGAN to learn an unknown Hamiltonian's approximate eigenstate from the real Hamiltonian. Results in the second experiment showed the QGEN's adversarial training outperformed the perfect swap test. However, the QDIS' approximations were off due to the entangled QGAN's lack of eigenstate phase estimation.

In the third experiment, [31] explored the efficiency of an entangled QGAN learning random states. As the QGEN variables are dynamic, ranging from two, four, or six qubits, and since the VQC only employs k-Nearest Neighbor interactions, [31] expected fidelity to increase parallel to qubit count; however, not all quantum gates performed the same. Instead, certain gates outperformed other gates, with some gates using two or fewer model layers. Thus, certain quantum gates presented a two-qubit gate advantage over simply increasing layers to the TFQ model.

While this new fully entangled QGAN developed by [38] showed promise at overcoming classically hard problems, [31] also noted that challenges rivaling traditional CGAN issues. Likewise, new QC-specific challenges were also presented with this new QGAN model as well. The next and final section of will perform a very simple experiment to test the accuracy and difficulty of the QML research explored throughout this chapter.

6. uQGAN noise model experimentation

This last section will perform a uQGAN experiment using IBM's Quantum Cloud, IBM Qiskit, IBM's extensive QC device framework, and Google's Tensorflow, which is fully supported on the IBM Quantum Cloud. All resources are accessible with minimal configuration, affording maximum development and experimentation time. This uQGAN leveraged IBM's original QGAN, updating IBM's now deprecated circuit quantum neural network (CircuitQNN) with IBM's newest sampler quantum neural network (SamplerQNN) QALGO, introduced May 2023 [43].

The original IBM QGAN lacked a noise model implementation, which was added to this uQGAN to accommodate QED/C experimentation. As such, a backend IBM SamplerAER noise model implementation was added to make it more difficult for the quantum discriminator to detect and correct superconducting-NISQ quantum errors. Lastly, the new uQGAN optimized the Tensorflow hyperparameters for the new SamplerQNN QALGO and noise model. The complete experiment can be retrieved in the Appendix.

This uQGAN will generate the real data from a quantum state. A quantum dataset rather than a classical dataset will be used. This synthetically created quantum mechanical dataset will be generated from a single VQC, with a qubit rotated from an initial ground state of $|0\rangle$ to an arbitrary fixed state. The uQGAN will then be tasked with learning a noise-injected generator circuit from an IBM SamplerAER Noise Model. It will be determined from training statistics, linear regression models, and other visualizations if the QGEN was able to reproduce the same (real data) quantum state for the fake data's generated quantum state. The goal of this experiment is to determine if a uQGAN is theoretically capable of decreasing QCERs in QIP by mechanizing QED/C.

Table 1 shows the hyperparameters used to train the uQGAN model in this experiment. It is important to remember that GANs comprise two independent models, as such the QGEN and QDIS need to be tuned separately and different optimizers may perform better for one over the other. Here, the best optimizer for the QGEN and QDIS was a stochastic gradient descent (SGD) optimizer, with a Learning Rate of 0.02. Next, 100 epochs, (the number of times all data in the quantum dataset is cycled through the QALGO) was used for the training run. The QGEN to QDIS step rates were set to one and five respectively. Thus, the QDIS updated its model five times for every one QGEN model update. The IBM SamplerAER Noise Model was used for this specific experiment, otherwise, all other hyperparameters were left at their default values.

Table 2 reveals the QGEN and QDIS cost estimates and KL Div. values for the uQGAN noise model independent variables. The lowest QGEN cost estimate for this experiment was −0.375 at Epoch 0, followed closely by −0.382 at Epoch 1. The highest QGEN estimate observed was −0.796 at Epoch 90. In turn, the lowest QDIS

	QGEN	QDIS
Optimizer	SGD	SGD
Learning Rate	0.02	0.02
Epoch	100	100
Steps	1	5
Noise Model	SamplerAER	SamplerAER

Table 1.
uQGAN model hyperparameters.

Epoch	Generator cost	Discriminator cost	KL Div.
0	−0.375	−0.454	1.33
10	−0.382	−0.585	1.36
20	−0.427	−0.57	1.39
30	−0.487	−0.514	1.4
40	−0.549	−0.453	1.41
50	−0.609	−0.393	1.41
60	−0.666	−0.336	1.41
70	−0.716	−0.286	1.39
80	−0.759	−0.243	1.38
90	−0.796	−0.206	1.35

Table 2.
Kullback-Leibler divergence (KL div.) measurement between the generator and discriminator.

cost estimate observed of −0.29 was also at Epoch 0. In turn, the QDIS' highest cost estimate was −0.206 was encountered at Epoch 90. The largest KL Div. value between the QDIS and QGEN was 1.41 between Epochs 40 and 60, while the smallest KL Div. value was 1.33 at Epoch 0.

The cost function is a measurement of how accurately the QGEN and QDIS models were in their ability to estimate their relationship between predicted values and their actual values. In turn, the KL Div value measures the distance between the uQGAN model's real and fake distribution. The lower the KL Div. value the higher the distribution's similarity. As such, a KL Div. value of zero indicates a distribution is equivalent. Therefore, the KL Div. values below indicate the QGEN and QDIS in this experiment are not equivalent.

Figure 1 shows the uQGAN training results for the QGEN and QDIS linear regression models. The visualization clearly shows the uQGAN model converge when the QGEN (blue) line intersects the QDIS (red) line around the −0.5 Loss mark. However, these results must be correlated against the KL. Div. values, in the subsequent line graph, which does not follow a zero trajectory.

Next, **Figure 2** shows that the trained quantum data distributions created by the uQGAN's QGEN are not equal to the real data distribution of a theoretical QC. This is visually apparent by reviewing the register mappings between the trained generator's distribution and the real distribution, as they are not identical. The trained generator

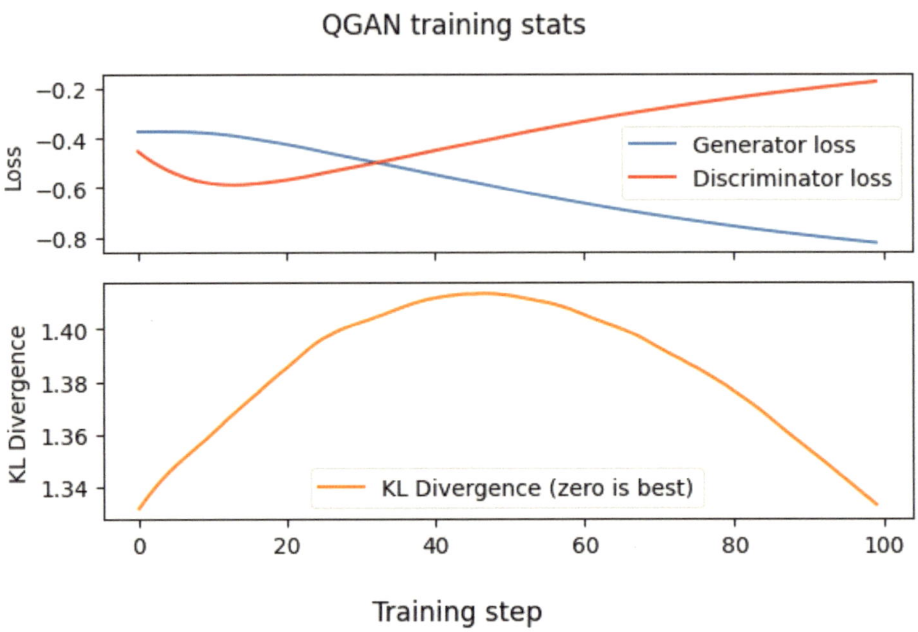

Figure 1.
Converged uQGAN noise model with KL div. and epoch.

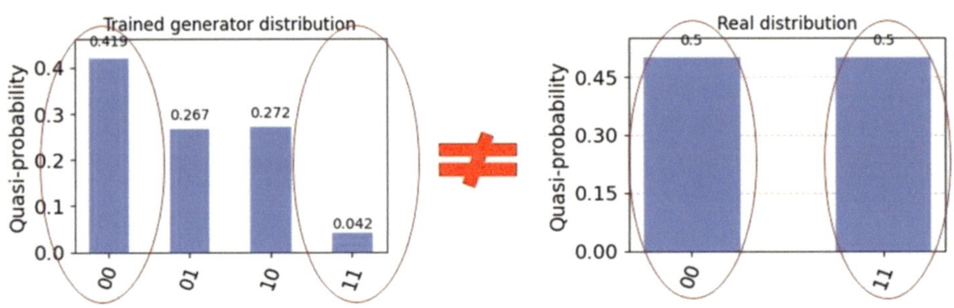

Figure 2.
Trained generator data distribution verses a real distribution from a perfect theoretical quantum computer.

distribution is the IBM QC device on the left, and while only qubits 00 and 11 were utilized by the program, two additional qubits were allocated to account for QEs, these are qubits 01 and 10. These will be excluded from the discussion below.

Next, regarding the quasi-probability of QIP success (00 or 11) verses QE (01 or 10) on the IBM QC, register 11 has the lowest quasi-probability rating at 0.042, while register (or qubit) 00 has the highest quasi-probability rating of 0.419. This is contrary to the theoretical QC which maintains a perfect quasi-probability score of 0.5 for both registers 00 and 11. These results indicate that the uQGAN failed to learn a VQC possessing an unknown state and reproduce that learned state on entangled qubits.

One additional result worth pointing out in **Figure 2**, with nearly all quantum data placed in qubit 00, a uQGAN mode collapse also certainly occurred. The trained generator's distribution is not balanced between the two quantum registers 00 and 11. As such, with nearly all the quantum data residing in qubit 00, the QDIS likely became too good at guessing the data.

DOI: http://dx.doi.org/10.5772/intechopen.1002876

7. Conclusions

This chapter commenced with a liberal overview of QIP, featuring QEs common to NISQ devices and the current lack of effective QED/C techniques for decoherence. Quantum error correction research was next discussed, with specific attention given to QML and its potential for QCER reduction. Quantum algorithms were next introduced, setting the groundwork for a thorough discussion of quantum GANs, both hybrid and fully entangled, with special attention given to uQGANs and their perceived applicability to future QECC strategies. The chapter concluded with a uQGAN Noise Model experiment compliments of IBM Quantum Cloud.

There were several key take-aways from this experiment, first, while the uQGAN did converge, closer inspection of the training statistics revealed that the KL Div. values were too high, indicating that the range between the QGEN and QDIS was too great, and the predictions were likely invalid. Thus, the model results were either inaccurate or simply occurred by chance.

Next, the trained generator's (fake) data distribution did not mirror the real distribution of a perfect QC. Instead, it indicated that the uQGAN was unlikely to mitigate detect and correct QEs by learning a VQC with an unknown state and reproducing its learned state on entangled qubits. Additionally, the observation of quantum data in register 11 was indicative of a mode collapse, indicating the discriminator likely became too good at guessing one type of data.

A great deal of content was covered in this chapter. It was intended to convey the immense amount of work that has gone into furthering the field of Quantum Machine Learning over the past several years. Quantum scale does not exist in a vacuum, it will not be achieved without quantum speed, which will not happen without mechanized quantum error correction.

Acknowledgements

Thank you to the IBM Quantum team, the Google AI Quantum team, and National University's School of Technology and Engineering's faculty and staff.

Conflict of interest

The author declares no conflict of interest.

Notes

The material used to create this chapter was derived from the author's Quantum Machine Learning Doctoral Dissertation. This work, however, was specifically crafted for the quantum-curious crowd, rather than the astute quantum research community.

A. Appendix

The Jupyter notebook containing all IBM Qiskit code from the Quantum experiment in this chapter can be retrieved from the following location: https://github.com/liv4unix/IntechOpenQML.

Author details

Theresa Melvin
TORII Technology Corporation, USA

*Address all correspondence to: theresa.melvin@toriitechnology.com

References

[1] Agliardi G, Prati E. Optimal tuning of quantum generative adversarial networks for multivariate distribution loading. Quantum Reports. 2022;**4**(1):75-105. DOI: 10.3390/quantum4010006

[2] Cai W, Ma Y, Wang W, Zou C, Sun L. Bosonic quantum error correction codes in superconducting quantum circuits. Fundamental Research. 2021;**1**(1):50-67. DOI: 10.1016/j.fmre.2020.12.006

[3] Swathi M, Rudra B. Novel encoding method for quantum error correction. In: 2022 IEEE 12th Annual Computing and Communication Workshop and Conference (CCWC). Jan 2022. pp. 1001-1005. DOI: 10.1109/CCWC54503.2022.9720880

[4] Biercuk MJ, Stace TM. Quantum error correction at the threshold: If technologists don't get beyond it, quantum computers will never be big. IEEE Spectrum. 2022;**59**(7):28-46. DOI: 10.1109/MSPEC.2022.9819881

[5] Chen SY, Yoo S. Federated quantum machine learning. Entropy (Basel, Switzerland). 2021;**23**(4):460. DOI: 10.3390/e23040460

[6] Hasan T, Ahmad F, Rizwan M, Alshammari N, Alanazi SA, Hussain I, et al. Edge caching in fog-based sensor networks through deep learning-associated quantum computing framework. Computational Intelligence and Neuroscience. 2022;**1-17**:6138434. DOI: 10.1155/2022/6138434

[7] Rodrigo S, Abadal S, Alarcon E, Almudever CG. Will quantum computers scale without inter-chip comms? A structured design exploration to the monolithic vs distributed architectures quest. In: 2020 XXXV Conference on Design of Circuits and Integrated Systems (DCIS). 2020. pp. 1-6. DOI: 10.1109/DCIS51330.2020.9268630

[8] Fan J, Li J, Wang Y, Li Y, Hsieh M, Du J. Partially concatenated Calderbank-Shor-Steane codes achieving the quantum Gilbert-Varshamov bound asymptotically. IEEE Transactions on Information Theory. 2022;**69**(1):262-272. DOI: 10.1109/TIT.2022.3201239

[9] Shor PW. Algorithms for quantum computation: Discrete logarithms and factoring. In: Proceedings 35th Annual Symposium on Foundations of Computer Science. Jan 1994. pp. 124-134. DOI: 10.1109/SFCS.1994.365700

[10] Qiskit. Quantum Generative Adversarial Networks. Available from: https://learn.qiskit.org/course/machine-learning/quantum-generative-adversarial-networks#quantum-5-0

[11] Murali P, Linke NM, Martonosi M, Abhari AJ, Nguyen NH, Alderete CH. Full-stack, real-system quantum computer studies: Architectural comparisons and design insights. In: 2019 ACM/IEEE 46th Annual International Symposium on Computer Architecture (ISCA). Jun 2019. pp. 527-540. Available from: https://search.ebscohost.com/login.aspx?direct=true&AuthType=sso&db=edseee&AN=edseee.8980312&site=eds-live&scope=site [Accessed: 17 October 2023]

[12] Nawaz SJ, Sharma SK, Wyne S, Patwary MN, Asaduzzaman M. Quantum machine learning for 6G communication networks: State-of-the-art and vision for the future. IEEE Access. 2019;**7**:46317-46350. DOI: 10.1109/ACCESS.2019.2909490

[13] Inada T, Jang W, Iiyama Y, Terashi K, Sawada R, Tanaka J, et al. Measurement-Free Ultrafast Quantum Error Correction by Using Multi-Controlled Gates in Higher-Dimensional State Space. Ithaca: Cornell University Library, arXiv.org; 2021. Available from Publicly Available Content Database https://search.proquest.com/docview/2568400022

[14] Locher GL. Photoelectric quantum counters for visible and ultraviolet light. Part I. Physical Review. 1932;**42**(4):525-546. DOI: 10.1103/PhysRev.42.525

[15] Deutscher M. Rigetti Debuts Multichip Quantum Processor with 80 Qubits. [SiliconANGLE]. 2021. Available from: https://siliconangle.com/2021/12/15/rigetti-debuts-multi-chip-quantum-processor-80-qubits/

[16] Rigetti Systems. Aspen-M-3 Quantum Processor. Available from: https://qcs.rigetti.com/qpus

[17] Martinis, J. & Boxio, S. Quantum Supremacy using a Programmable Superconducting Processor. 2019. Available from: https://ai.googleblog.com/2019/10/quantum-supremacy-using-programmable.html

[18] IBM Systems. Available from: https://www.ibm.com/quantum/systems

[19] Bertels K, Sarkar A, Hubregtsen T, Serrao M, Mouedenne AA, Yadav A, et al. Quantum computer architecture toward full-stack quantum accelerators. IEEE Transactions on Quantum Engineering. 2020;**1**:1-17. DOI: 10.1109/TQE.2020.2981074

[20] Ayanzadeh R, Dorband J, Halem M, Finin T. Multi-qubit correction for quantum annealers. Scientific Reports. 2021;**11**(1):16119. DOI: 10.1038/s41598-021-95482-w

[21] Terhal BM, Conrad J, Vuillot C. Towards scalable bosonic quantum error correction. IOP Publishing. 2020:19-20. DOI: 10.1088/2058-9565/ab98a5

[22] Nakaji K, Yamamoto N. Quantum semi-supervised generative adversarial network for enhanced data classification. Scientific Reports. 2021;**11**(1):19649. DOI: 10.1038/s41598-021-98933-6

[23] Kanamori Y, Yoo S-M. Quantum computing: Principles and applications. Journal of International Technology and Information Management. 2020;**29**(2):1

[24] Endo S, Cai Z, Benjamin SC, Yuan X. Hybrid quantum-classical algorithms and quantum error mitigation. Journal of the Physical Society of Japan. 2021;**90**(3):32001. DOI: 10.7566/JPSJ.90.032001

[25] Zhang S, Li L. A brief introduction to quantum algorithms. CCF Transactions on High Performance Computing. 2022;**4**(1):53-62. DOI: 10.1007/s42514-022-00090-3

[26] Hu X. Application of Moore's law in semiconductor and integrated circuits intelligent manufacturing. In: 2022 IEEE 2nd International Conference on Power, Electronics and Computer Applications (ICPECA). Jan 2022. pp. 964-968. DOI: 10.1109/ICPECA53709.2022.9719252

[27] Liu W, Zhang Y, Deng Z, Zhao J, Tong L. A hybrid quantum-classical conditional generative adversarial network algorithm for human-centered paradigm in cloud. EURASIP Journal on Wireless Communications and Networking. 2021;**2021**(1):1-17. DOI: 10.1186/s13638-021-01898-3

[28] Stein SA, Baheri B, Chen D, Mao Y, Guan Q, Li A, et al. QuGAN: A quantum state fidelity based generative adversarial

network. In: 2021 IEEE International Conference on Quantum Computing and Engineering (QCE). 2021. pp. 71-81. DOI: 10.1109/QCE52317.2021.00023

[29] Killoran N, Izaac J, Quesada N, Bergholm V, Amy M, Weedbrook C. Strawberry fields: A software platform for photonic quantum computing. Quantum. 2019;**3**:129. DOI: 10.22331/q-2019-03-11-129

[30] Saini S, Khosla P, Kaur M, Singh G. Quantum driven machine learning. International Journal of Theoretical Physics. 2020;**59**(12):4013-4024. DOI: 10.1007/s10773-020-04656-1

[31] Rasmussen SE, Zinner NT. Multiqubit State Learning with Entangling Quantum Generative Adversarial Networks. Ithaca: Cornell University Library, arXiv.org. Retrieved from Publicly Available Content Database; 2022. Available from: https://arxiv.org/abs/2204.09689

[32] Barbeau M, Garcia-Alfaro J. Faking and discriminating the navigation data of a micro aerial vehicle using quantum generative adversarial networks. In: 2019 IEEE Globecom Workshops (GC Wkshps). 2019. pp. 1-6. DOI: 10.1109/GCWkshps45667.2019.9024550

[33] Ali T, Jan S, Alkhodre A, Nauman M, Amin M, Siddiqui MS. DeepMoney: Counterfeit money detection using generative adversarial networks. PeerJ Computer Science. 2019;**5**:e216. DOI: 10.7717/peerj-cs.216

[34] Eckerli F, Osterrieder J. Generative Adversarial Networks in Finance: An Overview. Ithaca: Cornell University Library, arXiv.org; 2021. Available from Publicly Available Content Database https://arxiv.org/abs/2106.06364

[35] Zoufal C, Lucchi A, Woerner S. Quantum generative adversarial networks for learning and loading random distributions. NPJ Quantum Information. 2019;**5**(1):1-9. DOI: 10.1038/s41534-019-0223-2

[36] Kaur I, Lydia EL, Nassa VK, Shrestha B, Nebhen J, Malebary S, et al. Generative adversarial networks with quantum optimization model for mobile edge computing in IoT big data. Wireless Personal Communications. 2021:1565-1585. DOI: 10.1007/s11277-021-08706-7

[37] Huang K, Wang Z, Song C, Xu K, Li H, Wang Z, et al. Quantum generative adversarial networks with multiple superconducting qubits. NPJ Quantum Information. 2021;**7**(1):1-5. DOI: 10.1038/s41534-021-00503-1

[38] Niu MY, Zlokapa A, Broughton M, Boixo S, Mohseni M, Smelyanskyi V, et al. Entangling Quantum Generative Adversarial Networks. Ithaca: Cornell University Library, arXiv.org. Retrieved from Publicly Available Content Database; 2021. Available from: https://search.proquest.com/docview/2521810318

[39] Benedetti M, Garcia-Pintos D, Perdomo O, Leyton-Ortega V, Nam Y, Perdomo-Ortiz A. A generative modeling approach for benchmarking and training shallow quantum circuits. NPJ Quantum Information. 2019;**5**(1):45. DOI: 10.1038/s41534-019-0157-8

[40] He Z, Li L, Zheng S, Huang Z, Situ H. A conditional generative model based on quantum circuit and classical optimization. International Journal of Theoretical Physics. 2019;**58**(4):1138-1149. DOI: 10.1007/s10773-019-04005-x

[41] Huang Y, Li X, Zhu Y, Lei H, Zhu Q, Yang S. Learning unitary transformation by quantum machine learning model. Computers, Materials & Continua. 2021;**68**(1):789-803. DOI: 10.32604/cmc.2021.016663

[42] Hu L, Wu S, Cai W, Ma Y, Mu X, Xu Y, et al. Quantum generative adversarial learning in a superconducting quantum circuit. Science Advances. 2019;**5**(1):eaav2761. DOI: 10.1126/sciadv.aav2761

[43] Qiskit. Introducing Qiskit Machine Learning 0.6. 2023. Available from: https://medium.com/qiskit/introducing-qiskit-machine-learning-0-6-25186b57bf97

Chapter 5

A Tour of Adiabatic Quantum Computing

Nicholas R. Allgood

Abstract

Different types and approaches for using quantum mechanical events for computation have developed quickly with the quantum technology revolution. One of these, adiabatic quantum computing, uses the adiabatic theorem as a paradigm for computation. According to the adiabatic theorem, if conditions gradually change and a system is permitted to adjust its configuration (changing the probability density), the associated eigenstate will be of the final Hamiltonian if the system starts in an eigenstate of its initial Hamiltonian. Simply put, a quantum mechanical system that is subjected to rapidly changing and varying conditions, there isn't enough time for a function to adapt which leaves the spatial probability density unchanged. A closely related optimization process that utilizes the adiabatic theorem known as quantum annealing, finds a global minimum over a candidate set of solutions by processing quantum fluctuations. Quantum annealing is used primarily in combinatorial optimization problems where the search space is large and discrete, containing multiple local minima.

Keywords: adiabatic, quantum annealing, quantum tunneling, ising, qubo

1. Introduction

Quantum computing is the use of quantum mechanical phenomena as a model for computation. There are many different phenomena that occur in quantum mechanics which has lead to a variety of different types of quantum computing. Gate model quantum computing utilizes a series of *quantum gates* to form a *quantum circuit* that is then processed by a quantum computer. While the gate model is the "universal" model of quantum computing often seen as the "holy grail" where the idea is a gate model quantum computer can be equivalent to the laptop on one's desk. Adiabatic quantum computing is a model of quantum computing that relies on the adiabatic theorem for computations. The original form proposed by Max Born and Vladimir Flock states: "A physical system remains in its instantaneous eigenstate if a given perturbation is acting on it slowly enough and if there is a gap between the eigenvalue and the rest of the Hamiltonian's spectrum"[1]. In more common terms, a quantum

[1] https://link.springer.com/article/10.1007/BF01343193

mechanical system that has is influenced by gradually changing external variables will adept it's functional form, however, when influenced by rapidly changing conditions there is not enough time for the functional form to adapt which causes the spatial probability density to not change. Adiabatic quantum computing tends to be best suited for pure optimization problems, such as partitioning or traveling salesman. While it is possible to convert any problem to a format suitable for an adiabatic quantum computer, one has to take careful consideration to ensure the overhead of converting the problem does not outweigh the result.

2. Brief foundations of quantum mechanics

While other chapters may have covered in more detail some of the foundational building blocks of quantum mechanics (quantum states, superposition, entanglement) we will still provide a very brief overview on these topics.

- **Quantum states** are entities that contains the knowledge of a quantum mechanical system [1]. Theoretically, everything around us and interacting with us, is a quantum system. More practically speaking, a quantum state is a mathematical construct that represents all the possibilities that could happen within a given moment.

- **Superposition** is where a particle can be any of the possible quantum states at any given time. When we measure a particle that is in superposition the current state will *collapse* and provide a deterministic state [1]. In quantum computing terms, this corresponds to one getting a deterministic finite result. The interactions before and after a quantum state are what *influence* a quantum state to be in the desired state which contains the desired result with the highest probability.

- **Entanglement** is the phenomenon that occurs where you have a group of particles where their quantum states are intermixed such that one cannot determine the quantum state of one of aforementioned particles individually [1]. One very unique property of entanglement is that these particles can be separated by a very large distance. In terms of quantum computing, entanglement occurs between *qubits* when a quantum mechanical operator is performed on at least two more qubits. This is what allows quantum computers to be able to represent large amounts of data in a relatively minimal space.

- **Hamiltonian** is another formulation of Lagrangian mechanics formulated by Sir Rowan Hamilton [1]. The Hamiltonian of a system is an operator that contains the total energy of a system where total energy is comprised of kinetic and potential energy. The systems spectrum of energy (eigenvalues) is the set of possible outcomes that can be derived from a measurement of a systems total energy. In quantum computing, specifically with adiabatic quantum computing, this is the formulation that is used as the input of a quantum computer. One formulates their problem into a Hamiltonian and the quantum computer processes and returns a result. In *quantum annealing*, we are often attempting to minimize or maximize an objective function. As such the ideal solution corresponds with the lowest energy solution provided.

DOI: http://dx.doi.org/10.5772/intechopen.1002604

3. The adiabatic theorem

The adiabatic theorem states that gradually changing conditions will allow a quantum mechanical system to adapt it's configuration or having it's probability density modified. If a system starts in an eigenstate in a given initial Hamiltonian, it will end in the corresponding eigenstate of the final Hamiltonian [1].

We have a quantum mechanical system H starting at a time denoted t_0. This quantum mechanical system has the energy at the point in time t_0 as denoted via $H(t_0)$. $H(t_0)$ is in an eigenstate we can label $\psi(x, t_0)$. If this system is modified continuously this will result in the final Hamiltonian of the system $H(t_1)$ where t_1 is some later point in time. The time-dependant Schroedinger equation will dictate how the system evolves to the final state $\psi(x, t_1)$. To truly be adiabatic we need our time to approach infinity $t \mapsto \infty$. This tells us that our state $\psi(x, t_1)$ will be an eigenstate of the final Hamiltonian $H(t_1)$ with the configuration:

$$|\psi(x, t_1)|^2 \neq |\psi(x, t_0)|^2 \tag{1}$$

How close one can approximate an adiabatic process is dependant on the energy *gap* between $\psi(x, t_0)$ and it's adjacent states. The ratio of our time interval t to our evolution of our initial state $\psi(x, t_0)$ for the *time-independent* equation is $2\pi\hbar/E_0$ where E_0 is the energy of our initial state $\psi(x, t_0)$. If we move in the other direction of our time scale where $t \mapsto 0$ the configuration of our state is unchanged and remains:

$$|\psi(x, t_1)|^2 = |\psi(x, t_0)|^2 \tag{2}$$

4. Adiabatic quantum computing

Now that we have briefly covered the adiabatic thereom we can further discuss adiabatic quantum computing, a model of quantum computing that follows the adiabatic theorem. One starts with a Hamiltonian where the *ground state* of this Hamiltonian is the solution to a specific problem. More specifically, this is often referred to as a *final Hamiltonian*. A simpler Hamiltonian, known as an *initial Hamiltonian* is prepared on a quantum system with its initial configuration being the ground state. The quantum system adiabatically evolves this Hamiltonian towards the configuration of the final Hamiltonian. This follows along with what is stated by the adiabatic theroem and the quantum system remains in the ground state. The system in the ground state corresponds with the solution to our problem ans has been shown to be polynomially equivalent to gate model quantum computing [2].

Time complexity for adiabatic quantum computing algorithms is a bit tricky as they are based on the time it takes for a Hamiltonian to adiabatically evolve in a quantum system. This is further tied to the *spectral gap*, also known as the energy eigenvalues of the Hamiltonian. We can state that if a system is kept at its ground state the spectral gap between the ground state and the first excited state of our Hamiltonian H for a time period of t, $H(t)$ will provide an upper bound at which the Hamiltonian can be evolved for time t [3]. The total runtime for our algorithm is bounded by:

$$T = O\left(\frac{1}{s_{min}^2}\right) \tag{3}$$

where s_{min} is the minimal spectral gap of $H(t)$.

Adiabatic quantum computing will solve many combinatorial search problems and Boolean satisfiability problems. These problems in particular are those that wish to have a state that solves $S_1 \wedge S_2 \wedge, \ldots, \wedge S_n$. This expression contains the Boolean satisfiability of the S statements where each statement S_i can only be true or false. This expression further uses n qubits where each qubit is a variable $x_k \in \{0, 1\}$ so that S_i is a Boolean value function of $x_1, x_2, \ldots, x_k$.

5. Quantum annealing

Quantum annealing is a heuristic optimization process for finding a global minimum (or maximum) for an objective function over a given set of candidate solutions [4]. These candidate solutions are in reality candidate quantum states and are obtained using quantum fluctuations. Quantum annealing specializes in problems with a discrete search space with many local minima. The current form in use today by most quantum annealers was originally proposed as a quantum-inspired classical algorithm [5].

Quantum annealing initially starts from a superposition of all possible states, each with equal weights. The system evolves following the time-dependant Schrödinger equation where the amplitudes of the candidate states are constantly changing, achieving a quantum parallelism. This quantum parallelism is dependant on the traverse (magnetic) field which causes a phenomenon known as *quantum tunneling* through the various peaks that are encountered. If the changing of the traverse field is slow enough, stays close to the ground state of the final Hamiltonian, however, if the traverse field is changed at a quicker rate, the system may leave this ground state briefly. While leaving the ground state even for a short period may seem detrimental, doing so produces a higher probability of ending up in the ground state of the final Hamiltonian. The traverse field is then removed and the system is anticipated to have reached the ground state which corresponds to a true global minimum. The classical Ising Hamiltonian is a model that corresponds to the solution of the original optimization problem.

5.1 Quantum tunneling

Adiabatic quantum computing and specifically quantum annealing rely heavily on the quantum mechanical phenomena known as quantum tunneling. Quantum tunneling simply put is the ability for a particle to penetrate through a potential energy barrier despite lacking enough energy as stated by classical mechanics. Simply put when a particle reaches a barrier most of that particle is reflected back from whence it came, however, some of that particle is transmitted through to the other side of the barrier. From a computation perspective, the larger our sets of data grow there are many "peaks and valleys" among the data as seen in the **Figure 1**.

These peaks and valleys in sets of data correspond to different *local minima* of the problem. Often as data sets grow exponentially large, they are subject to what is known as the *local minima problem*. The local minima problem is where an algorithm attempts to "climb" out of deep valley or minima but doesn't do so when the processing stops. This local minima may or may not be the global minima of the set of data. By leveraging quantum tunneling, we are able to tunnel through the variety of peaks and valleys and settle on a true global minimum that corresponds with the lowest energy state.

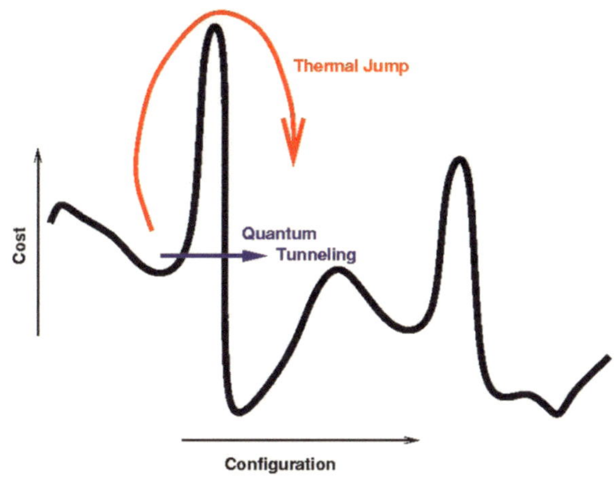

Figure 1.
Quantum tunneling [6].

5.2 Formulations

Theoretically there a variety of different Hamiltonians that can be used with adiabatic quantum computing, however, the Ising Hamiltonian is the most common and often only Hamiltonian supported by many adiabatic quantum computers. The Ising model is a mathematical model of ferromagnetism in statistical mechanics created by Ernst Ising and Wilhelm Lenz. The model contains discrete variables that represent moments of magnetic dipoles where the atoms can be in a *spin up* or *spin down* state which corresponds to +1 for spin up and −1 for spin down. We represent the formulation as the following Hamiltonian:

$$\mathcal{H}_{ising} = -\frac{A(s)}{2}\left(\sum_i \sigma_x^i\right) + \frac{B(s)}{2}\left(\sum_{i>j} J_{i,j}\sigma_z^i\sigma_z^j\right) \tag{4}$$

where σ are Pauli matrices operating on a specific qubit, A and B are energy scaling functions, h_i are qubit biases and J_i are coupling strengths or *chains* between qubits.

An equivalent and slightly more computer science friendly formulation is known as the Quadratic Unconstrained Binary Optimization (QUBO). QUBO is specifically a combinatorial optimization problem with a wide variety of applications and formulations for common NP-hard problems. Let B^n be a set of binary vectors with a fixed length where $n > 0$ and $B = \{0, 1$ is the set of values used by bits. Given an upper triangular matrix $Vin\mathbb{R}^{nxn}$ where entries V_{ij} are the weight for each pair of indices within the binary vector. We define a function$f_V : B \mapsto \mathbb{R}$ that will assign a value to each binary vector. This is accomplished through the equation:

$$f_V(x) = x^{\mathrm{T}}Vx - \sum_{i=1}^{n}\sum_{i=j}^{n} V_{ij}x_ix_j \tag{5}$$

With this established, the QUBO problem finds a binary vector x' that is minimal tof_V or:

$$x' = \arg\min_{x \in B^n} f_V(x) \tag{6}$$

As mentioned, the QUBO formulation is computationally equivalent to the Ising Hamiltonian, with the biggest difference is the QUBO formulation uses 0 to represent a spin down and a 1 to represent a spin up.

6. Hardware and software platforms

There are a few vendors for adiabatic quantum computing with the biggest and most well-known being D-Wave [7]. D-Wave has been developing adiabatic quantum computers since 1999. They provide a limited but free access to some of their quantum computers which they refer to as *solvers*. D-Wave offers a *hybrid* solver which relies on a proprietary process to determine which of your problem will be computed by a classical CPU and which parts will be computed using the quantum CPU. In addition to the Hybrid solver, as part of this offering D-Wave's quantum solver is either a Binary Quadratic Model (BQM), Constrained Quadratic Model (CQM), or Discrete Quadratic Model (DQM).

The biggest limitation is the amount of time one's problem can run on the quantum CPU of their solvers. D-Wave does offer a developer account where you synchronize an open source code repository to your account and you are afforded more time and possibly access to more solvers. They use an API cloud based system known as LEAP where you submit your quantum programs via an API call. The software platform that is utilized by D-Wave is known as the Ocean SDK. The SDK is only available in the Python programming language and makes submitting quantum programs to their solvers quite simple to perform. Much care and thought must be taken when formulating your problem and *embedding* it as a QUBO or Ising formulation, for which D-Wave supports both.

In addition to D-wave, NEC also offers a quantum annealing hardware. While not explicitly a quantum annealer, Fujitsu, Hitachi, and NIT have offerings that are classical but support the Ising formulation of an optimization problem. Microsoft Azure through Azure quantum is another offering that is available that supports an Ising formulation through Microsoft's cloud offering. It should be noted that Microsoft, Amazon, etc cloud providers often provide a *service* to leverage quantum computing, but behind the scenes they often have a wide variety of quantum computing vendors include gate model machines. Fujitsu also offers a digital annealer which is a quantum-inspired classical annealer.

A simple test program using D-Wave's Ocean SDK is below. This program uses an Ising formulation.

```
import dimod
from dwave.system.composites import EmbeddingComposite
from dwave.system.samplers import DWaveSampler
h = {}
J = {(225, 261): 0.0, (127, 19): 0.0 }
sampler = EmbeddingComposite(DWaveSampler())
sampleset = sampler.sample_ising(h, J, num_reads=1000)
print(sampleset)
print(sampleset.first.sample)
```

We take note of the results printed below. the **print(sampleset)** prints all of the available solutions with their respective energies with the lowest energy on top.

19	127	225	261	energy	num_oc.	chain_.
0	-1	-1	-1	+1	0.0	37	0.0
1	-1	-1	+1	-1	0.0	69	0.0
2	+1	+1	+1	-1	0.0	80	0.0
3	+1	-1	-1	-1	0.0	39	0.0
4	-1	-1	+1	+1	0.0	88	0.0
5	+1	+1	-1	+1	0.0	47	0.0
6	+1	+1	+1	+1	0.0	85	0.0
7	-1	-1	-1	-1	0.0	32	0.0
8	+1	+1	-1	-1	0.0	53	0.0
9	-1	+1	-1	-1	0.0	49	0.0
10	-1	+1	+1	-1	0.0	96	0.0
11	-1	+1	+1	+1	0.0	103	0.0
12	-1	+1	-1	+1	0.0	53	0.0
13	+1	-1	+1	+1	0.0	70	0.0
14	+1	-1	+1	-1	0.0	61	0.0
15	+1	-1	-1	+1	0.0	38	0.0

['SPIN', 16 rows, 1000 samples, 4 variables]

The **print(sampleset.first.sample)** is the solution that corresponds to the lowest energy only.

```
{19: -1, 127: -1, 225: -1, 261: 1}
```

7. Applications of adiabatic quantum computing

Adiabatic quantum computing can be applied to any problem, however it is definitely more suitable for combinatorial optimization problems. D-Wave has a large number of case studies located at https://www.dwavesys.com/learn/resource-library/. To highlight a few, Recruit Group is utilizing quantum annealing to optimize television commercials to time-slots. SavantX has been using quantum annealing to optimize logistics at the Port of Los Angeles, boasting a 60% increase in crane deliveries per crane during a working day. Multiverse computing has been utilizing quantum annealing in the financial sector to optimize financial portfolios. D-Wave solvers have also been used in the pharmaceutical industries to accelerate drug discovery.

Fujitsu's digital annealer has a few case studies associated with it which also are primarily optimization problems in a variety of fields. A full list of these case studies can be found at https://www.fujitsu.com/global/services/business-services/digital-annealer/what-is-digital-annealer/. One of these case studies is utilizing the digital annealer in manufacturing with the optimization of robotic arm movements. Robotics are getting more and more complex as technology and society evolve so naturally the complexity of the tasks we require of robotics also increases. In addition to D-Wave, Fujitsu is also utilizing their digital annealer and working with drug research companies to accelerate drug discovery.

Though not being used in production, the author's own research is good example of utilizing quantum annealing for a practical problem in cluster analysis. Cluster analysis are a set of algorithms used to statistically group items closer together by how they are related to each other. There are many types of clustering algorithms that are in heavy use today, one such being known as *prototype based clustering*. This style of clustering has a center point known as a *centroid* for which all other data points in a cluster are related too in some way, shape, or form. Picking the starting center point when a clustering algorithm begins is a difficult sub-problem and often chosen at random. While this has proven to be effective, there is still a risk at starting with a non-optimal random selection thus increasing convergence time. Quantum Optimized Centroid Initialization (QOCI) was developed to assist with this problem by leveraging quantum annealing to further optimize initial starting centroids [8]. Utilizing the principles of adiabatic quantum computing, QOCI relies on minimizing a constrained objective function to obtain a true global minimum. Once that global minimum is found, the resulting data is post processed into cluster centroids.

8. Conclusion

While there appears to be a lot of unnecessarily augmented claims about the advance of quantum computing, many of these claims are specific to gate model quantum computing. It's well known that even with the great strides we have made in research, gate model quantum computing still has quite a long road ahead before it starts to permeate into society. Adiabatic quantum computing appears to be further along in terms of being a more practical quantum computing solution with many companies already utilizing quantum annealing in production to improve their day to day business operations. In the above chapter we have explored just a few of many case studies involving D-Wave and how they have optimized a variety of business customers.

Usually, adiabatic quantum computers boast a much larger number of qubits than gate-model computers, however, it should be noted that the quality of the qubits is of equal importance. As such a new metric known as *quantum volume* was created in 2018 and redefined by IBM in 2019. Quantum volume factors in error rates into noisy qubits which exist on both gate-model and adiabatic quantum computers. Adiabatic quantum computing might be considered limited by some, however there are plenty of practical uses for adiabatic quantum computing and with more being developed every day. The ongoing research of both gate model and adiabatic quantum will continue to be mutually beneficial in the present and the future.

Author details

Nicholas R. Allgood
University of Maryland Baltimore County, USA

*Address all correspondence to: allgood1@umbc.edu

References

[1] Sakurai JJ. Modern Quantum Mechanics. 2nd ed. San Francisco, CA: Pearson Education, Inc., Publishing as Addison-Wesley; 2004

[2] Dorit A, Wim v D, Julia K, Zeph L, Seth L, Oded R. Society for industrial applied mathematics (SIAM). SIAM Review. 2008;**2008**:755-787

[3] van Dam W, Mosca M, Vazirani U. How powerful is adiabatic quantum computation? In: Proceedings 42nd IEEE Symposium on Foundations of Computer Science. 8-11 Oct 2001. p. 279

[4] Finnila AB, Gomez MA, Sebenik C, Stenson C, Doll JD. Quantum annealing: A new method for minimizing multidimensional functions. Chemical Physics Letters. 1994;**1994**:343-348

[5] Kadowaki T, Nishimori H. Quantum annealing in the transverse Ising model. Physical Review E. 1998;**58**:5355-5363

[6] Das A, Chakrabarti BK. *Colloquium*: Quantum annealing and analog quantum computation. Reviews of Modern Physics. Sep 2008;**80**(3):1061-1081

[7] D-Wave. Available from: https://www.dwavesys.com/

[8] Allgood NR, Borle A, Nicholas CK. Quantum Optimized Centroid Initialization. arXiv ePrint 2305.08626. Available from: https://arxiv.org/abs/2305.08626 [Accessed: July 23, 2023]

Chapter 6

Practical Applications of Quantum Computing

Esam El-Araby, Manu Chaudhary, Ishraq Ul Islam, David Levy, Dylan Kneidel, Mingyoung Jeng, Alvir Nobel and Vinayak Jha

Abstract

With the rapid advancement of quantum computing technology, there is a strong motivation to explore suitable practical applications for quantum algorithms and quantum computers. This chapter focuses on reviewing recent research on practical applications of quantum computing, specifically dimension reduction, pattern recognition, quantum sorting, and quantum communications for which optimized/modified versions of the quantum wavelet transform (QWT) and Grover's algorithm are presented. For practical implementations of the presented algorithms, this chapter also includes methodologies for classical-to-quantum (C2Q) data encoding and quantum-to-classical (Q2C) data decoding. Additionally, the chapter presents an efficient quantum sorting technique by combining perfect-shuffle and bitonic networks. In the domain of quantum communications, the chapter reviews a technique that combines chaotic communications with quantum key distribution (QKD) to enhance both security and communication range. The effectiveness of these techniques is validated through practical results obtained from experiments conducted on IBM-Q simulators and hardware, as well as on high-performance-reconfigurable-computers (HPRCs). This chapter aims to provide readers with a comprehensive understanding of these applications, covering the necessary prerequisites by showcasing the potential of quantum computing in various domains for innovative problem-solving.

Keywords: quantum computing, quantum algorithms, quantum encoding, quantum decoding, quantum communications

1. Introduction

Quantum computing is a field at the forefront of technological innovation. It promises significant speedup over classical computation in certain workloads, largely due to its inherent parallelism [1], enabled by quantum mechanical properties such as superposition and entanglement [2]. State-of-the-art quantum processors, called Noisy Intermediate-Scale Quantum (NISQ) devices, are limited by their relatively few qubits and susceptibility to noise and decoherence effects [3]. *Decoherence* is the process through which the state of a quantum computer is destroyed by unintended interactions with the environment [4] and is, therefore, an especially critical challenge for current NISQ devices. Moreover, quantum algorithms that require deep quantum circuits take a longer time to run and exacerbate the impact of decoherence [5]. These limitations make practical implementations of complex quantum algorithms quite challenging.

This chapter sets out to present and review existing research efforts that demonstrate some practical applications of quantum computing. On a high level, quantum computations generally consist of three stages: (1) data input/encoding, (2) data processing, and (3) data output/decoding. This chapter has thus been organized roughly in that same flow. More specifically, Section 2 describes a technique for encoding data into the quantum domain from the classical domain, termed as classical-to-quantum (C2Q) data encoding, while Section 3 describes algorithm development and optimization for quantum systems, and Section 4 discusses some techniques for quantum-to-classical (Q2C) data decoding. In addition, Section 5 explores research in quantum communications that combines chaotic communications with quantum key distribution (QKD) for enhancing both security and communication range. Finally, Section 6 concludes the chapter with closing remarks.

2. Classical data encoding

Prior to executing quantum algorithms, particularly for data-intensive applications, data must be encoded from the classical domain into the quantum domain. The process of initializing qubits with a quantum state corresponding to arbitrary classical data is called *data encoding, state preparation,* and/or *arbitrary state synthesis* [6–8]. There are three main techniques for encoding classical data into quantum domain: (1) *basis encoding*, (2) *angle encoding*, and (3) *amplitude encoding* [9]. Among the different data encoding methods, amplitude encoding requires the least number of qubits [10]. This technique encodes data as the probability amplitudes (coefficients) of the basis states into a quantum superposition. This section presents a depth optimized amplitude encoding technique with up to 50% reduction in circuit depth and total gate count compared with closest competing alternative [6]. This technique is termed as classical-to-quantum (C2Q) data encoding [10].

2.1 Classical-to-quantum (C2Q) data encoding

For a classical dataset of $N = 2^n$ elements, where n is the number of required qubits, an n-qubit quantum state $|\psi\rangle$ can encode each data element as a probability amplitude/coefficient C_i of a basis state $|i\rangle$. The C2Q method [11] can be used to synthesize $|\psi\rangle$ from the ground state $|\psi_0\rangle = |0\rangle^{\otimes n}$ using a unitary operator U^{C2Q}, see Eq. (1).

$$\begin{aligned} |\psi\rangle &= U^{C2Q} \cdot |\psi_0\rangle = U^{C2Q} \cdot |0\rangle^{\otimes n} \\ &= \sum_{i=0}^{N-1} C_i |i\rangle, \text{ where} \sum_{i=0}^{N-1} |C_i^2| = 1 \end{aligned} \tag{1}$$

The state $|\psi\rangle$ of a single qubit can be visualized using a Bloch sphere of global scale $r = 1$, global phase t, azimuth angle ϕ, and elevation angle θ. To initialize $|\psi\rangle$ from the ground state $|0\rangle$, the *ZYZ* or Pauli decomposition can be used to apply a rotation of

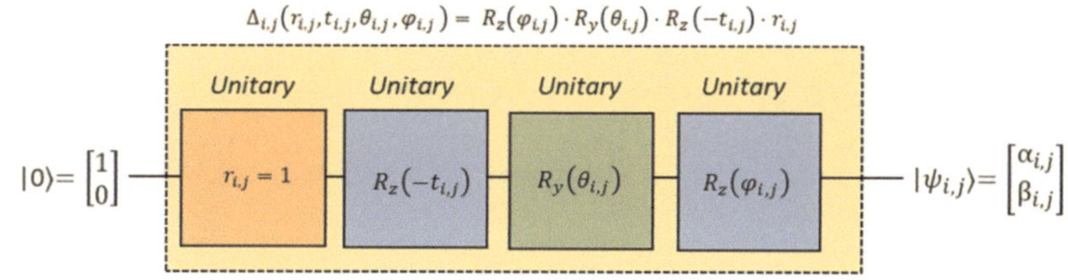

Figure 1.
Pauli (ZYZ) decomposition for single-qubit state synthesis [10].

angle $-t$ around the z-axis, followed by another rotation of angle θ around the y-axis, and finally a rotation of angle ϕ around the z-axis, see **Figure 1** and Eq. (2). Conversely, the parameters t, θ, and ϕ in Eq. (2) can be derived from the state coefficients α and β using Eq. (3),

$$\begin{aligned} |\psi\rangle &= C_0|0\rangle + C_1|1\rangle = \alpha|0\rangle + \beta|1\rangle \\ &= R_z(\phi)\cdot R_y(\theta)\cdot re^{\frac{it}{2}}\cdot|0\rangle \\ &= R_z(\phi)\cdot R_y(\theta)\cdot R_z(-t)\cdot r\cdot|0\rangle \end{aligned} \tag{2}$$

$$t = \angle\beta + \angle\alpha, \quad \theta = 2\tan^{-1}\left(\frac{|\beta|}{|\alpha|}\right), \quad \phi = \angle\beta - \angle\alpha, \tag{3}$$

where $|\alpha| = \sqrt{Re^2(\alpha) + Im^2(\alpha)}$, $\angle\alpha = \cos^{-1}\left(\frac{Re(\alpha)}{|\alpha|}\right)$, $|\beta| = \sqrt{Re^2(\beta) + Im^2(\beta)}$ and $\angle\beta = \cos^{-1}\left(\frac{Re(\beta)}{|\beta|}\right)$.

To synthesize an arbitrary multi-qubit state from the ground state $|\psi_0\rangle = |0\rangle^{\otimes n}$, an operation U_j^{C2Q}, see **Figure 2**, can be used to iteratively synthesize the entangled state of the j-th qubit in the output state, where $0 \le j < n$. U_j^{C2Q} is composed of $k_j = 2^{(n-1-j)}$ conditional $\Delta_{i,j}$ rotation operations, where $0 \le i < k_j$. Thus, U_j^{C2Q} can be represented by a block-diagonal matrix, where each diagonal block is a 2×2 transformation matrix $\Delta_{i,j}$, see Eq. (4). Block-diagonal matrices such as U_j^{C2Q} can be implemented using a uniformly-controlled circuit or a quantum multiplexer [6]. In this approach, the target qubit, i.e., the least-significant qubit, is subjected to various gates or operations for every possible combination of the control qubits. In **Figure 2**, the 'square box' notation [6] is used for the control bits, and the parameterized operations on the data qubit are replaced by a single box denoting the operation. The overall transformation U^{C2Q} from the ground state $|\psi_0\rangle = |0\rangle^{\otimes n}$ to $|\psi\rangle$ can be expressed by Eq. (5), also see **Figure 3**.

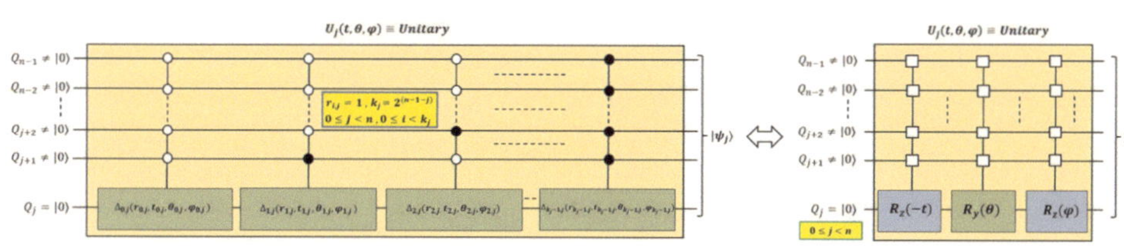

Figure 2.
Multiplexer (conditional-logic) quantum circuit [10].

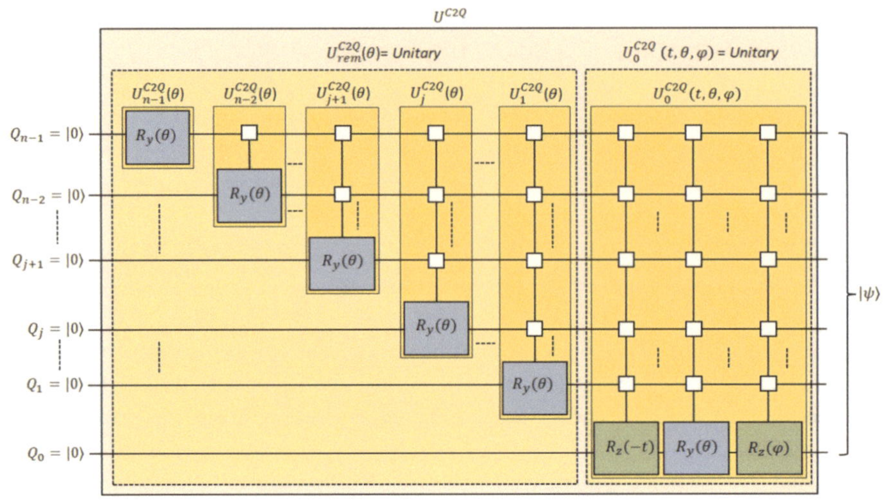

Figure 3.
Quantum circuits for unitary C2Q data encoding [10].

$$\begin{aligned} U_j^{C2Q} &= \Delta_{0,j} \oplus \Delta_{1,j} \oplus \cdots \Delta_{i,j} \cdots \oplus \Delta_{(k_j-1),j} \\ &= \text{diag}\left(\Delta_{0,j}, \Delta_{1,j}, \cdots, \Delta_{i,j}, \cdots, \Delta_{(k_j-1),j}\right) \end{aligned} \tag{4}$$

$$\begin{aligned} U^{C2Q} &= U_0^{C2Q}(t,\theta,\phi) \cdot \left(\prod_{j=1}^{n-1} U_j^{C2Q}(\theta) \otimes I^{\otimes j} \right) \\ &= U_0^{C2Q}(t,\theta,\phi) \cdot U_{rem}^{C2Q}(\theta) \end{aligned} \tag{5}$$

As shown in **Figure 1**, each $\Delta_{i,j}$ operation requires calculating a 2-tuple with parameters $(\alpha_{i,j}, \beta_{i,j})$ from the given classical data set $|\psi\rangle$. These parameters are determined by following the steps detailed in Eq. (6) to Eq. (8). Subsequently, they are utilized in Eq. (3) to derive the 4-tuple parameters $(r_{i,j}, t_{i,j}, \theta_{i,j}, \phi_{i,j})$. It is important to emphasize from Eq. (6) to Eq. (8), that the transformation retains its unitarity, where $r_{i,j} = \sqrt{|\alpha_{i,j}|^2 + |\beta_{i,j}|^2} = 1$.

$$P_{i,j} = \begin{cases} |C_{2i}|^2 + |C_{2i+1}|^2, & j = 0,\ 0 \le i < 2^{(n-1)} \\ P_{2i,j-1} + P_{2i+1,j-1}, & 1 \le j < n,\ 0 \le i < 2^{(n-1-j)} \\ 0, & 2^{(n-1-j)} \le i < 2^{(n-1)} \end{cases} \tag{6}$$

$$\alpha_{i,j} = \begin{cases} \dfrac{C_{2i}}{\sqrt{P_{i,j}}}, & P_{i,j} \neq 0,\ j = 0,\ 0 \le i < 2^{(n-1)} \\ \sqrt{\dfrac{P_{2i,j-1}}{P_{i,j}}}, & P_{i,j} \neq 0,\ 1 \le j < n,\ 0 \le i < 2^{(n-1-j)} \\ 1, & P_{i,j} = 0 \end{cases} \tag{7}$$

$$\beta_{i,j} = \begin{cases} \dfrac{C_{2i+1}}{\sqrt{P_{i,j}}}, & P_{i,j} \neq 0,\ j = 0,\ 0 \leq i < 2^{(n-1)} \\ \sqrt{\dfrac{P_{2i+1,j-1}}{P_{i,j}}}, & P_{i,j} \neq 0,\ 1 \leq j < n,\ 0 \leq i < 2^{(n-1-j)} \\ 0, & P_{i,j} = 0 \end{cases} \tag{8}$$

where $0 \leq j < n$, $0 \leq i < k_j$, and $k_j = 2^{(n-1-j)}$. The derivations of circuit depths and experimental results can be found in [10].

3. Algorithm development and optimization

This section introduces the readers to recent research work on some practical applications of quantum computing. The techniques presented here are (1) dimension reduction, (2) pattern recognition, and (3) quantum sorting.

3.1 Dimension reduction

The dimension reduction of multi-dimensional data is an area of great interest but it presents a formidable computational challenge for current classical systems. For example, wavelet-based techniques have proven effective for dimension reduction [12, 13], but they are still computationally expensive. The quantum wavelet transform (QWT), specifically the quantum Haar transform (QHT) [12, 14], offers a potential solution for dimension reduction due to its inherent parallelism. Presented here are multidimensional and multilevel-decomposable QHT techniques used for dimension reduction in both packet and pyramidal form.

3.1.1 Quantum wavelet transform (QWT)

The wavelet transform (WT) decomposes signals/data into its spatio-temporal spectral components [13]. The first and the simplest wavelet transform, called the Haar wavelet transform [15], is constructed using a unit step function $u(t)$, see Eq. (9). The discretized version of the Haar wavelet function, see Eq. (10), can also be implemented in the quantum domain. The general discrete quantum wavelet transform (QWT) [12] can be expressed by (12), where Ψ_D is the discretized Haar mother wavelet function, Δt denotes the sampling period, K is the window size of the wavelet in samples, $N = 2^n$ is the total number of data samples expressed as quantum basis-states, n represents the number of qubits, $|\psi\rangle$ stands for the input state, and $|\psi\rangle_{\text{QWT}}$ represents the output state.

$$\Psi(t)_{Haar} = u(t) - 2u\left(t - \frac{1}{2}\right) + u(t-1) \tag{9}$$

$$\Psi_D\left(\frac{i}{N}\right) = \begin{cases} +1, & 0 \leq i \leq \dfrac{N}{2} \\ -1, & \dfrac{N}{2} \leq i \leq N \\ 0, & \text{otherwise} \end{cases} \tag{10}$$

$$|\psi\rangle = \sum_{q=0}^{N-1} f(q\cdot\Delta t)|q\rangle, \text{ where} \sum_{q=0}^{N-1} |f(q\cdot\Delta t)|^2 = 1 \tag{11}$$

$$|\psi\rangle_{\text{QHT}} = \frac{1}{\sqrt{N}}\sum_{j=0}^{N-1}\sum_{q=0}^{N-1} f(q\cdot\Delta t)\Psi_D\left(\frac{q-j}{K}\right)|j\rangle \tag{12}$$

3.1.2 Rotate-left (RoL) and rotate-right (RoR) operations

Quantum RoL and RoR gates [16] are specifically designed permutation operations constructed using SWAP gates. Each gate executes a cyclic rotation, i.e., perfect-shuffle, of input qubits, through a series of $n-1$ SWAP gates over n qubits, see **Figure 4**.

3.1.3 QHT circuits

The QHT algorithm is multilevel-decomposable [16], represented by a generalized d-dimensional operation, denoted as $U^{d-D-QHT}$, see **Figure 5a**. When multi-dimensional data is encoded into the state amplitudes, a subset of continuous n_i qubits is required to represent the ith dimension of the data, where $0 \le i < d$. $U^{d-D-QHT}$ performs a single level of decomposition over all d dimensions in parallel, see **Figure 5a**. In this algorithm, a Hadamard (H) gate is applied to the least-significant qubit of each dimension to retrieve the low and high frequency components from the input data. Subsequently, an RoR operation is applied to separate the low-frequency components from those with high-frequencies [18].

The depth δ of the $U^{d-D-QHT}$ operation is determined by the depth of the critical path across all dimensions, see Eq. (13). The execution time t taken by $U^{d-D-QHT}$ to run on a quantum hardware can be approximated by using the gate delay times of the H and SWAP gates, denoted by τ_{H} and τ_{SWAP}, respectively. In terms of space complexity metric, the total gate count γ can be expressed by Eq. (15), derived from **Figure 5a**.

$$\delta = \max(\{1 + (n_i - 1) : i \in \mathbb{Z}, 0 \le i < d\}) = n_{\max} \tag{13}$$

$$t = \tau_{\text{H}} + (\delta - 1)\cdot\tau_{\text{SWAP}} \tag{14}$$

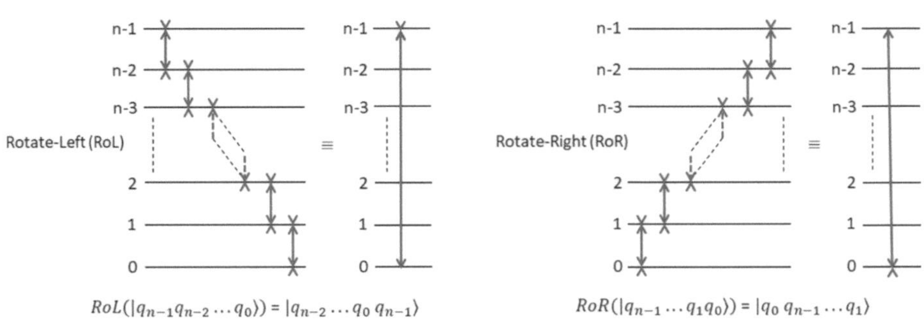

Figure 4.
Rotate-left (RoL) and rotate-right (RoR) gates [16].

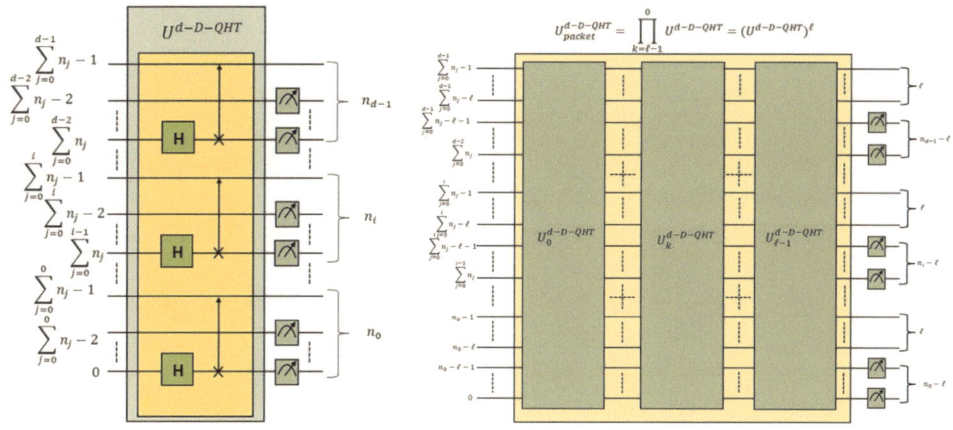

(a) (b)

Figure 5.
Circuits for QHT decomposition [17]. (a) Single-level decomposition of d-dimensional QHT. (b) ℓ-level, d-dimensional packet decomposition.

$$\begin{aligned}\gamma &= \sum_{i=0}^{d-1}(1\mathrm{H}-\mathrm{gate}+(n_i-1)\mathrm{SWAP}-\mathrm{gate}) \\ &= d\mathrm{H}-\mathrm{gate}+(n-d)\mathrm{SWAP}-\mathrm{gate}=n\ \mathrm{gates}\end{aligned} \tag{15}$$

Interleaved packet decomposition: In the multilevel packet decomposition variant of QHT, the $U^{d-D-QHT}$ operation is applied repeatedly to all qubits at each decomposition level, see **Figure 5b**. The equations used to determine the hardware execution time and the circuit depth by applying $U^{d-D-QHT}$ operations in series are presented in [16] and [18]. However, the circuit depth can be further minimized by the overlapping the H gates and the SWAP gates across multiple decomposition levels. This technique, known as interleaving the $U^{d-D-QHT}$ operations, allows these gates to be executed concurrently, resulting in an overall reduction in circuit depth [17]. The optimized packet decomposition circuit employs two extra layers of SWAP gates for each added interleaved level of decomposition, as shown in Eqs. (16) and (17). The expression for total gate count γ_{pkt} for the multilevel packet decomposition QHT circuit, see Eq. (18), is derived from Eq. (15) and **Figure 5b**.

$$\delta_{pkt} = n_{\max}+2(\ell-1) \tag{16}$$

$$\begin{aligned}t_{pkt} &= \tau_{\mathrm{H}}+(n_{\max}+\ell-2)\cdot\tau_{\mathrm{SWAP}}+(\ell-1)\cdot\max(\tau_{\mathrm{H}},\tau_{\mathrm{SWAP}}) \\ &= \tau_{\mathrm{H}}+\left(\delta_{pkt}-1\right)\cdot\tau_{\mathrm{SWAP}}\end{aligned} \tag{17}$$

$$\gamma_{pkt} = n\cdot\ell \tag{18}$$

Interleaved pyramidal decomposition: In pyramdial decomposition, the $U^{d-D-QHT}$ operation is applied to a reduced number of data qubits (d fewer qubits), reducing by one qubit for each dimension. Although this reduction in qubits can lead to shallower circuit compared to packet decomposition, it necessitates additional interlevel

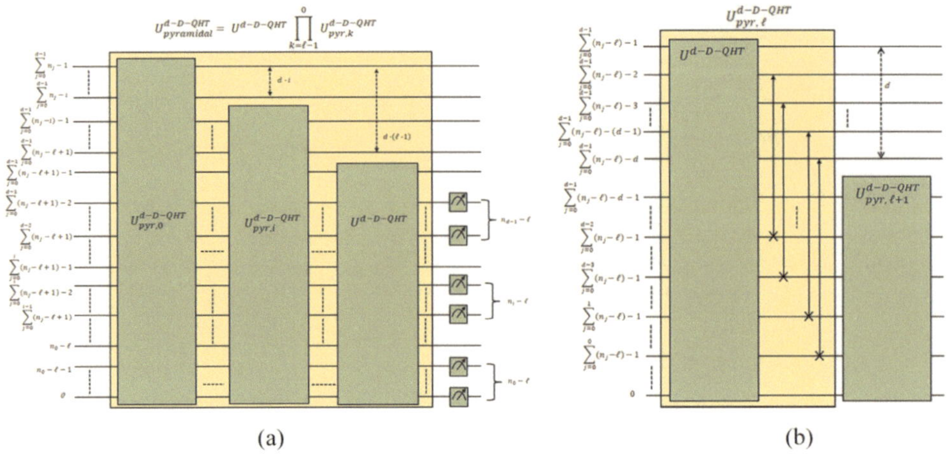

Figure 6.
ℓ-level, d-dimensional pyramidal decomposition [17]. (a) Structure of pyramidal decomposition. (b) Interlevel permutations.

permutations to maintain data locality among the different decomposition levels, as shown in **Figure 6b**.

The pyramidal decomposition operation also supports interleaving. When interleaving is applied at the second decomposition level ($\ell = 2$), additional layers of gates, i.e., $n - n_{\max} - d + 2$ layers, are appended to the first decomposition level. The first level is composed of $U^{d-D-QHT}$ operation and interlevel permutations. On adding each subsequent decomposition level, i.e., $\ell > 2$, an extra d gate layers are added to the total circuit depth. The overall depth of interleaved pyramidal decomposition is described by Eq. (19) and the execution time is expressed by Eq. (20).

$$\delta_{pyr} = \begin{cases} n_{\max}, & \ell = 1 \\ n + d(\ell - 1) - 2(d - 1), & \ell > 1 \end{cases} \tag{19}$$

$$t_{pyr} = \tau_{\mathrm{H}} + \left(\delta_{pyr} - 1\right) \cdot \tau_{\mathrm{SWAP}} \tag{20}$$

The total gate count, denoted as γ_{pyr}, for the multilevel pyramidal decomposition is determined using **Figure 6** and is expressed by Eq. (21), where n_0 denotes the number of required qubits for the first dimension. However, the pyramidal structure reduces the gate count required for the packet decomposition by a factor $\sum_{i=0}^{\ell-1}(d \cdot i) = \frac{d \cdot \ell \cdot (\ell - 1)}{2}$, see **Figure 6a**, while requiring additional gates $\gamma_{pyr-perm}$, for interlevel permutations as shown in **Figure 6b** and expressed by Eq. (22).

$$\gamma_{pyr} = \gamma_{pkt} + \gamma_{pyr-perm} - \frac{d \cdot \ell \cdot (\ell - 1)}{2}, \text{where} \tag{21}$$

$$\gamma_{pyr-perm} = \frac{d \cdot (\ell - 1)}{2} \left(n - n_0 - \frac{\ell \cdot (d - 1)}{2}\right) \tag{22}$$

Figure 7a and **b** show a $(64 \times 64 \times 3)-$pixel input image and the corresponding output image after 1-level of 3D-QHT, respectively. **Figure 7c** presents the output

DOI: http://dx.doi.org/10.5772/intechopen.1003033

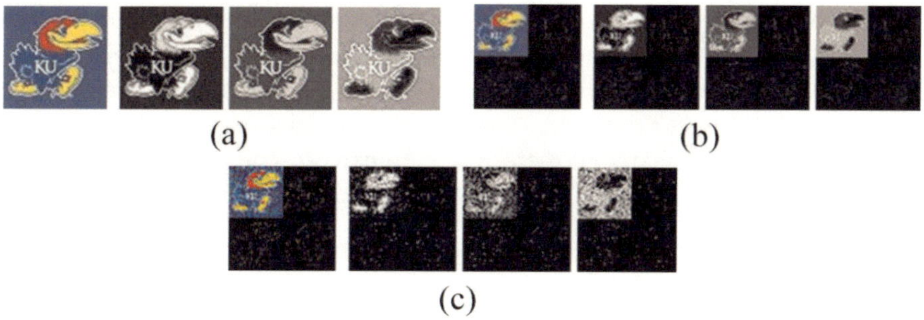

Figure 7.
Dimension reduction on (64 × 64 × 3)-pixel RGB images using 1-level 3D-QHT [16]. (a) Original RGB images. (b) Output images from MATLAB simulations. (c) Output images from IBM-Q simulations.

image reconstructed from IBM-Q simulations of 1-level 3D-QHT. For comprehensive experimental evaluations, please refer to [16].

3.2 Pattern recognition

Pattern recognition on multi-dimensional data is a challenging problem to solve using classical computers. In domains dealing with multi-dimensional data, not all measured components are relevant for detecting the area of interest. An effective pre-processing method would involve techniques of dimension reduction [19] of the data for faster processing and matching. Wavelet-based dimension reduction techniques [13, 15] are effective in data pre-processing, reducing computation overhead, and improving classification accuracy. This section presents a pattern recognition technique that uses optimized versions of QWT and quantum Grover's search (QGS) for time-efficient single-pattern/multi-pattern search in high-dimensional datasets.

3.2.1 Pattern recognition using quantum dimension reduction

The methodology of pattern recognition using multiple decomposition levels of 2D-QHT as a pre-processing step, see **Figure 8a**, is implemented as cascaded packet wavelet transforms, see also Section 3.1.1. A pattern matching search is then performed on the dataset with low spatial resolution using multi-pattern Grover's search. In this approach, the input classical data is encoded into the N basis states of a superimposed quantum state [11] utilizing a set of $n = \lceil \log_2 N \rceil$ qubits. Using L decomposition levels of 2D-QHT, the input dataset is converted to a low spatial resolution data consisting of

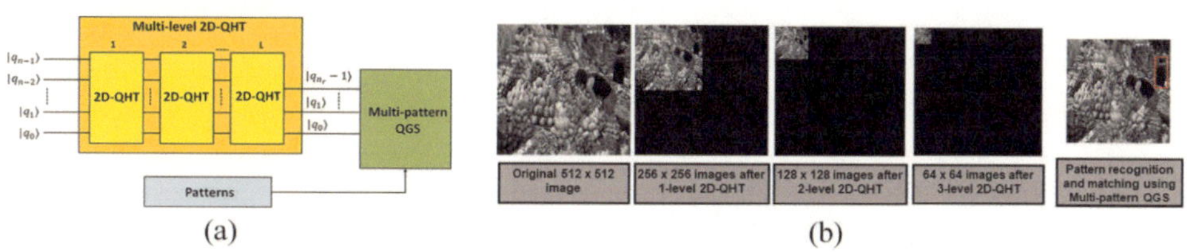

Figure 8.
Pattern recognition using quantum dimension reduction [20]. (a) Overview of methodology for pattern recognition using dimension reduction [20]. (b) Pattern recognition using quantum dimension reduction on a (512 × 512)-pixel image.

N_r quantum basis states. Here, $L = \lfloor \frac{1}{2} \log_2 \frac{N}{N_r} \rfloor$, N_r is pre-determined quantum data resolution less than N. The N_r reduced data is represented with n_r qubits, on which a search to find a number of patterns/basis states $N_{patterns}$ is performed. Thus, the multilevel 2D-QHT reduces the dimensionality of the data and the multipattern QGS returns the indices of the searched pattern, see **Figure 8b**. The use of this technique yields faster results compared to classical dimension reduction and search methods [20].

3.2.2 Quantum Grover's search algorithm

The quantum Grover's search algorithm is used to find an element s^* in an unordered N element set $S = \{s_1, s_2, s_3, \dots, s_N\}$, that makes $f(s^*) = 1$. Here, N is the cardinality of S, and f is a boolean function such that $f(x) \rightarrow \{0, 1\}$. A quantum computer running Grover's algorithm can provide a quadratic speedup [21] compared to classical counterparts.

Grover's oracle and Grover's diffusion: In QGS algorithm, in order to search an element in an unordered set, the essential steps involve performing the *operations of phase inversion* (oracle) and *inversion about the mean* (diffusion). These operations are performed for an optimal number of iterations. The oracle operation flips the sign of the target pattern's state while leaving the other states unchanged. It is represented as $U_{oracle}|x\rangle = (-1)^{f(x)}|x\rangle$. The diffusion operation amplifies any inverted coefficients and attenuates other coefficients [22]. This operation is represented as $U_{diffusion} = I - 2|x\rangle\langle x|$. The $U_{diffusion}$ is performed by calculating the mean of all the amplitudes, followed by inverting the value of each amplitude with respect to the mean. This results in reducing the amplitudes that are larger than the mean while amplifying the ones that are smaller [11].

3.2.3 Multi-pattern quantum search

The design and methodology of the modified/optimized multi-pattern Grover's search algorithm is shown in **Figure 9**. The first key modification involves the addition of a dynamic oracle circuit denoted as U_{oracle}, which efficiently identifies items

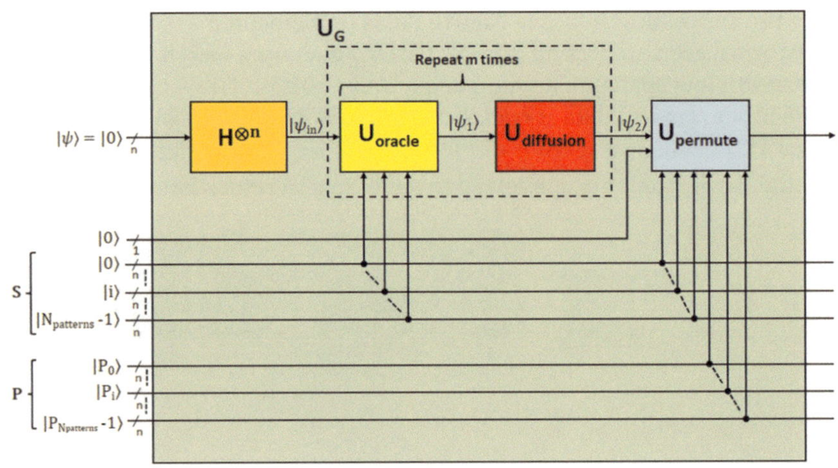

Figure 9.
Modified quantum circuit for multi-pattern Grover's algorithm [23].

positioned at the first $N_{patterns}$ indices in the search list. This is followed by the application of a diffusion circuit $U_{diffusion}$, which increases the probabilities of locating the pattern(s). The second modification incorporates a permutation operation, referred to as $U_{permute}$, which utilizes ancilla qubits for encoding and assigning probability coefficients to the corresponding basis states. This step is critical for successfully locating the target pattern(s).

The modified quantum circuit for multi-pattern Grover's algorithm, see **Figure 9** has four inputs:

- a collection of n compute qubits that are all initialized to the state $|\psi\rangle = |0\rangle$,
- a flag ancilla qubit, configured to the ground state $|0\rangle$,
- a collection of $N_{patterns}$ entries of statically initialized n ancilla qubits, i.e., $S = \{|0\rangle, |1\rangle, \ldots, |N_{patterns-1}\rangle\}$, and
- a collection of $N_{patterns}$ entries consisting of n ancilla qubits that can be dynamically changed. These qubits represent the input patterns that needs to be sought and amplified in $|\psi_{in}\rangle$, i.e., $P = \left\{|P_0\rangle, |P_1\rangle, \ldots, |P_{N_{patterns-1}}\rangle\right\}$.

After applying the H gate, the input qubit state vector $|\psi_{in}\rangle$ is expressed as $|\psi_{in}\rangle = \frac{1}{\sqrt{N}}\sum_{i=0}^{N-1}|i\rangle$. After putting the input qubits in superposition, a modified dynamic oracle operator U_{oracle} and an unmodified diffusion operator $U_{diffusion}$ are applied m times to amplify the first $N_{patterns}$ states. The optimal number of iterations, m is determined using Eq. (23) where $k = 1,3,5,7, \ldots$ is an odd number. Since, only the initial $N_{patterns}$ are amplified, a permutation operation, denoted as $U_{permute}$ is required to assign higher amplitudes to the target states based on input patterns P. The final output state is derived by performing these repeated iterations and the complete process can be represented by a single unitary matrix, denoted as $U_G = \left(U_{diffusion} \cdot U_{oracle}\right)^m$. The probability $P_{success}$ of successfully finding a desired pattern in the final output state $|\psi_{out}\rangle$ is expressed in Eq. (24) [24], where $N_{patterns} \leq N$.

$$m = \left\lfloor \frac{\pi \cdot \mathrm{k}}{4\sin^{-1}\left(\sqrt{\frac{N_{\mathrm{patterns}}}{N}}\right)} \right\rfloor \tag{23}$$

$$\begin{aligned} P_{success} &= \sin^2((2m+1) \times \theta), \\ \theta &= \sin^{-1}\left(\sqrt{\frac{N_{patterns}}{N}}\right), \text{and } 0 < \theta \leq \frac{\pi}{2} \end{aligned} \tag{24}$$

Modified oracle and diffusion circuits: The modified oracle circuit U_{oracle} uses *CNOT* gates to dynamically modify the target patterns as seen in **Figure 10a** and **b**. This dynamic search pattern modification extends the algorithm's capabilities to search for any pattern using a single quantum circuit. The *CNOT* gates within each oracle are efficiently controlled using ancilla qubits by adjusting them to the current pattern $|i\rangle$, see **Figure 10a**. For multi-pattern search, cascaded and incremental single-

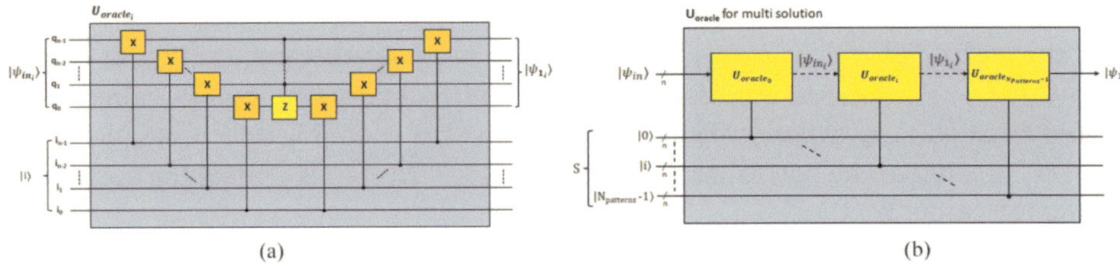

Figure 10.
Modified Grover's oracle for single and multiple solutions/pattern [23]. (a) Single solution/pattern. (b) Multiple solutions/patterns.

pattern oracle quantum circuits are applied to invert the first $N_{patterns}$ amplitudes as depicted in **Figure 10b**. The output of the oracle is provided to the diffusion circuit for amplification. The U_{oracle} and $U_{diffusion}$ are then iterated over m times to maximize the target amplitudes.

Quantum state permutation: In the modified design of Grover's algorithm, the amplitudes of the first $N_{patterns}$ states are amplified, and an additional permutation step assigns these amplitudes to the target basis states within the output state $|\psi_{out}\rangle$. For a detailed study of the permutation circuit, please refer to [23].

3.3 Quantum sorting

Another interesting application of quantum computing is sorting. This section presents the quantum implementation of the bitonic sort [25]. The bitonic sort is a comparison-based sorting algorithm that leverages *bitonic sequences* and is suitable for parallel implementations [26]. For an unordered sequence of N elements, it has a spatio-temporal complexity of $O(N\log^4 N)$ [26]. However, the optimized implementations using the *perfect shuffle* technique have shown to have a spatio-temporal complexity of $O(N\log^2 N)$ on a sequential processor and a complexity of $O(\log^2 N)$ on a system with N parallel processors [26]. When implemented on a quantum computer, the complexity improves to $O(n\log^2 n)$ [25], where $n = \lceil \log_2 N \rceil$ and n is the number of qubits.

3.3.1 Bitonic sort and perfect shuffle

Bitonic sequences [27] are sequences of elements which first increase monotonically in value and then decrease monotonically. A bitonic sequence can be expressed as $x_0 \leq \cdots \leq x_i \geq \cdots x_{n-1}$ where $0 \leq i < n$. Sequences sorted in ascending order or descending order are also considered bitonic sequences with zero elements on the descending side and ascending side respectively.

The classical version of the algorithm works by taking in an unsorted input sequence and recursively creating and merging smaller bitonic sequences into larger sequences until the whole list is eventually sorted. The bitonic sort algorithm is modeled as a *sorting network* [27] which uses *comparator* circuits that compare two input elements (x_0, x_1) and produces an output sequence $(\max(x_0, x_1), \min(x_0, x_1))$ or $(\min(x_0, x_1), \max(x_0, x_1))$ based on how the comparator is configured.

A quantum implementation of the comparator [25] takes two qubits, $|q_0\rangle$ and $|q_1\rangle$, and a mode qubit as inputs and if the mode qubit is $|0\rangle$ sets $|q_0\rangle = \min(q_0, q_1)$ and

$|q_1\rangle = \max(q_0, q_1)$. Similarly, if the mode qubit is set to $|1\rangle$, it sets $|q_0\rangle = \max(q_0, q_1)$ and $|q_1\rangle = \min(q_0, q_1)$. An implementation of such a comparator circuit is provided in **Figure 11**.

The *perfect shuffle* [28] technique improves the temporal complexity of a bitonic sort, which helps against the decoherence constraints on a quantum computer. A perfect shuffle intersperses elements of two equal length sequences, so that each element in the first group is followed by the corresponding element at the same position in the second group. The *quantum perfect shuffle* (QPS) [25] is a quantum implementation of a perfect shuffle that leverages the fact that a cyclical left shift on the indexes of a sequence of elements, expressed in their binary form, performs the equivalent of a perfect shuffle on the elements of that sequence. The quantum perfect shuffle can be implemented by a series of SWAP gates, identical to the RoL circuit shown in **Figure 4**.

3.3.2 Quantum bitonic sort with perfect shuffle

Data is encoded into a quantum circuit with n qubits using amplitude encoding [11] and follows Algorithm 1.1. The algorithm operates in m stages, where $m = \log_2(n)$. At each stage t, $m - t$ QPS operations are performed, followed by t QPS-comparison pairs, see **Figure 12**. A QPS-comparison pair is a QPS operation followed by a comparison operation, which is the application of a set of comparators between two adjacent qubits, see **Figure 11**.

For $t = 1$, the comparators are applied with their modes following an alternating *min-max* (mode 0) and *max-min* (mode 1) pattern, which can be represented as $[0,1,0,1,\cdots]$. For each subsequent stage $1 < t < m$, the pattern begins as $[0,1,0,1,\cdots]$ for the first QPS-comparison pair and is quantum perfect-shuffled before each of the following QPS-comparison pairs in the same stage. Finally, when $t = m$, the comparator pattern is $[0,0,0,0,\cdots]$ and no perfect shuffle of the pattern is necessary. The

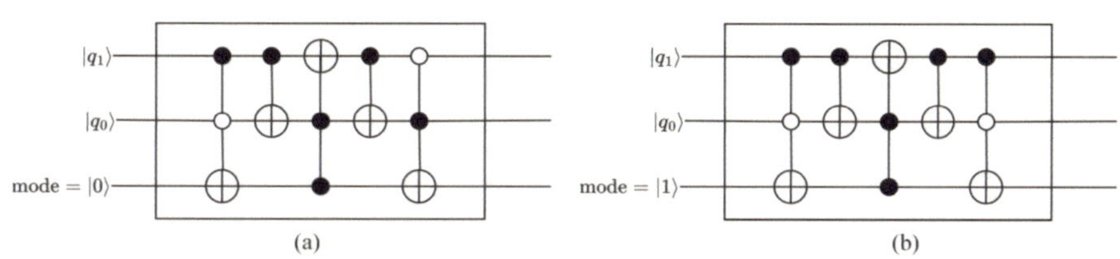

Figure 11.
Quantum comparator circuits [25]. (a) Quantum Comparator Circuit, Mode 0. (b) Quantum Comparator Circuit, Mode 1.

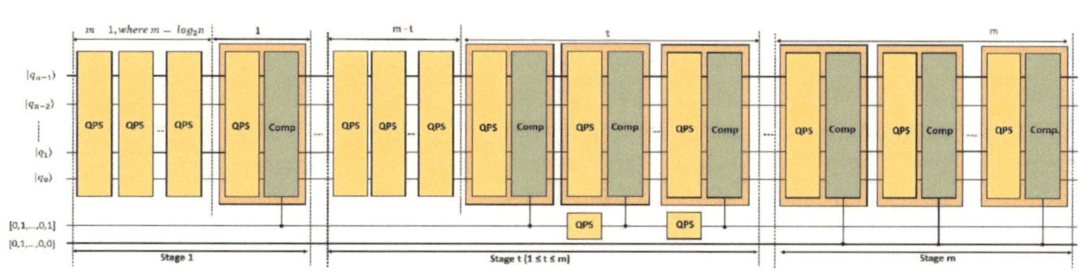

Figure 12.
Quantum circuit for combined bitonic sort with perfect shuffle permutation [25].

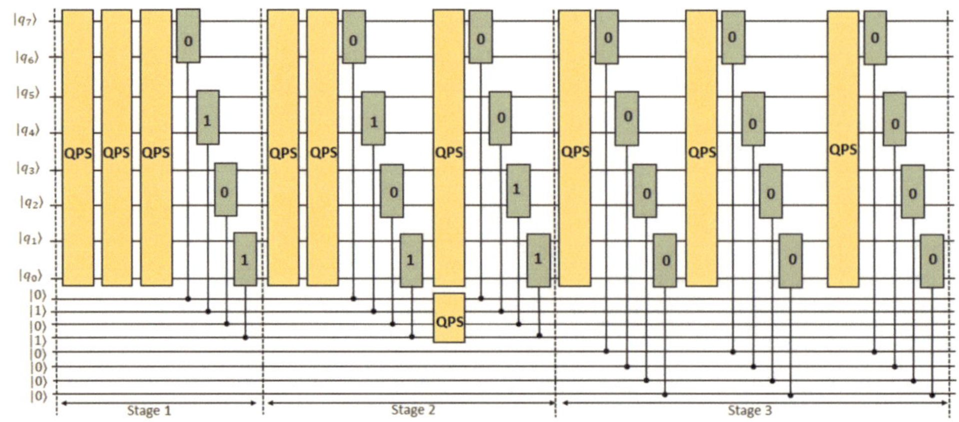

Figure 13.
Example of an 8-qubit quantum bitonic sorter [25].

general structure of the algorithm is provided in **Figure 12** and an example circuit for an 8-qubit bitonic sorter is given in **Figure 13**.

Algorithm 1.1: Bitonic sort with perfect shuffle.

```
for t in range (1, m):
    mode(t)
    for i in range (1, m − t):
        QPS(qubits)
    end for
    for i in range (m − t + 1,m):
        QPS(qubits)
        comparator (qubits, mode)
        QPS(mode)
    end for
end for
```

---

4. Quantum-to-classical (Q2C) data decoding

The process of decoding classical information from a quantum computer output can be a complex and time-consuming process. This critical challenge [3] limits the practical applications of existing Noisy Intermediate-Scale Quantum (NISQ) devices [29]. For example, in applications like quantum image processing data is usually represented using state amplitudes [30]. In such cases, to retrieve the processed image data from its quantum representation, it is necessary to sample the quantum circuit repeatedly, creating a probability distribution [31]. This operation, known as quantum-to-classical (Q2C) data decoding, introduces a substantial time overhead during circuit execution, promoting the need for further exploration of time-efficient methods for data decoding.

Traditional data decoding methods, as depicted in **Figure 14a** acquire the entire quantum state by repeated circuit sampling, often referred to as circuit 'shots'. In

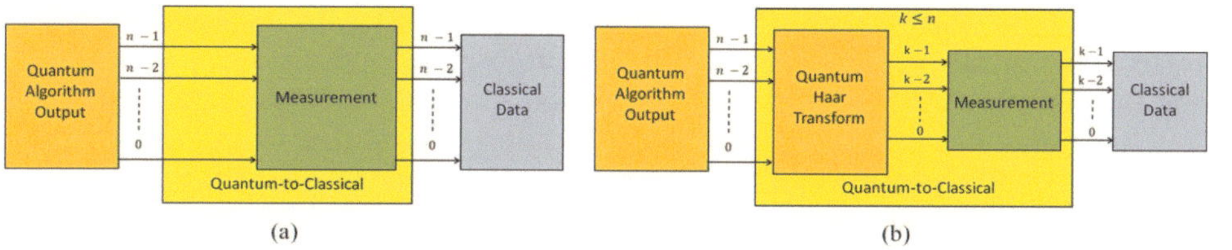

Figure 14.
Q2C data decoding using conventional and QHT-based methods [17]. (a) Conventional Q2C data decoding. (b) QHT-based Q2C data decoding.

general, a substantial number of repeated circuit samples are required to enhance the measurement accuracy and to reduce the impact of statistical noise. Consequently, this significantly increases the total time required for circuit execution.

To minimize the overhead of repeated circuit sampling, algorithms which decrease either the number of measured qubits or the number of required shots can be added to the circuit immediately prior to measurement. One effective technique for reducing the number of measured qubits is the multilevel-decomposable QHT [17]. By using this approach, data initially represented by n qubits can be transformed into a representation using fewer qubits, specifically $k = n - (\ell \cdot d)$, where $0 \leq k \leq n$, $0 \leq \ell \leq (n/d)$ represents the number of decomposition levels, and

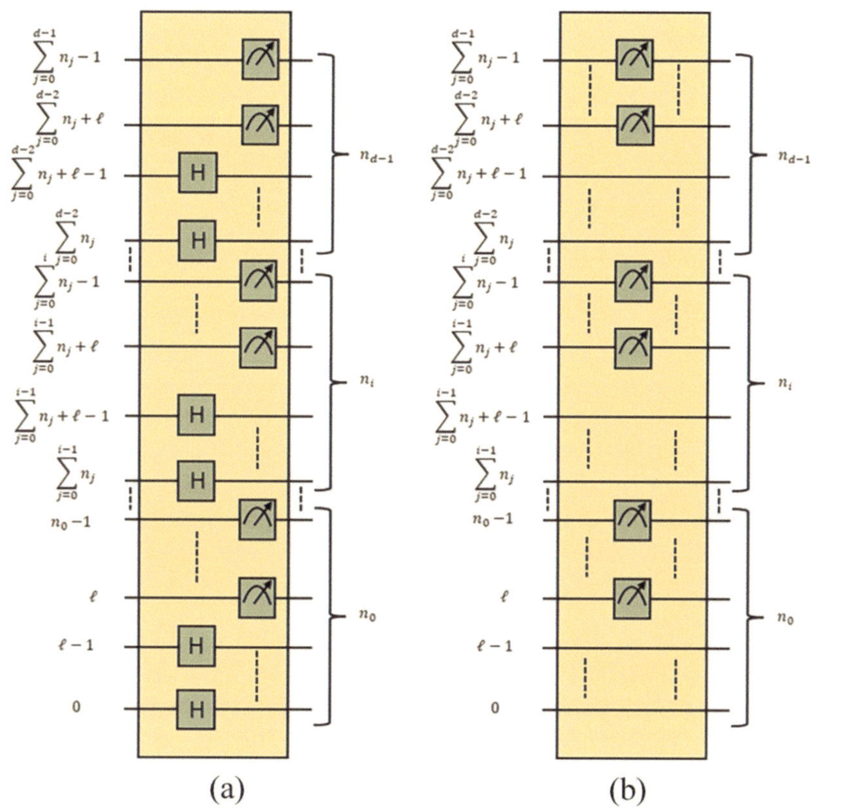

Figure 15.
ℓ-level, d-dimensional measurement-based decomposition [17]. (a) Single-gate depth with H gates. (b) Zero-depth circuit.

$d \geq 1$ is the data dimensionality, see **Figure 14b**. Another depth-optimized method, known as the 'measurement-based' QHT decomposition, operates effectively without using the additional quantum circuit [17]. In this method, the measurement of selectively lower number of qubits enables the sampling of output data within a lower-dimensional space. The two QHT-based circuits which can be used for Q2C data-decoding are multilevel packet and multilevel pyramidal decomposition circuits of QHT, see **Figures 5** and **6** and Section 3.1.3 for details. The 'measurement-based' QHT decomposition circuit is shown in **Figure 15**. Please refer to [17] for a detailed study of different Q2C circuits, their mathematical expressions and experimental evaluations.

5. Chaotic and quantum communications

In today's interconnected world, ensuring the security of transmitted data remains a challenging problem. Current communication systems rely on classical cryptographic methods to safeguard data privacy. However, these approaches are susceptible to potential threats posed by future quantum computers capable of breaking cryptographic algorithms. This concern has spurred significant interest in exploring quantum communication solutions. This section presents a Free-space optical (FSO) communication scheme that combines chaotic communication and Quantum Key Distribution (QKD) to enhance both range and security compared to currently used FSO methods. This approach employs auto-synchronizable Lorenz chaotic transmitter and receiver models to produce chaotic signals as data carriers. Utilizing the chaotic communication techniques, the data is sent securely over the classical channel, while QKD ensures a secure exchange of critical parameters used for synchronization over the quantum channel. This section illustrates the combination of chaotic communication and QKD to establish an end-to-end encrypted Deep-Space optical communications link.

5.1 Chaotic communications

In conventional communication systems, a carrier signal is required to carry information. For successful communication, the transmitter and receiver need to be synchronized. However, chaotic communication systems use a different approach. Instead of using a periodic carrier signal, they use chaotic signals. These systems can self-synchronize when driven by a common signal [32]. One example of such a chaotic system is the Lorenz chaotic system [33], represented as the Lorenz attractor. It can be split into two stable response subsystems, and both subsystems can synchronize with the original system, facilitating robust and secure communication.

5.2 Quantum key distribution (QKD)

QKD is a highly secure method of distributing cryptographic keys between two parties using the principles of quantum mechanics. Unlike conventional cryptographic methods that rely on the complexity of algorithms, QKD's security is based on fundamental laws of physics. QKD works by encoding a private key as a quantum state (qubits) and sending it over a quantum channel [34]. If an eavesdropper tries to intercept the qubits, it will alter their states due to the fundamental characteristics of quantum mechanics [34]. The BB84 protocol [35], introduced by Bennett and

Brassard in 1984, is one of the earliest and most widely used QKD protocols. It uses photons' polarization properties to transmit the key information, establishing a secure key between two communicators.

5.3 Communication system combining chaotic systems with QKD

The communication system presented consists of a transmitter (TX) and a receiver (RX), communicating through classical and quantum channels. The process begins when the QKD transmitter (TX) and receiver (RX) exchange chaotic synchronization parameters using a two-way BB84-like protocol employing both quantum and classical channels. The QKD RX model retrieves these chaotic parameters and provides them to the Lorenz chaotic receiver, as shown in **Figure 16**. The system uses digital modulation, error correction, and decoding techniques to achieve reliable communication over the Additive White Gaussian Noise (AWGN) channel. The hardware circuits of the transmitter and receiver are presented in **Figure 17**. For details about the preshaped codebook used for encrypting/decrypting data, see **Figure 18** and refer to [36]. In the study of cryptographic methods for secure communication, some

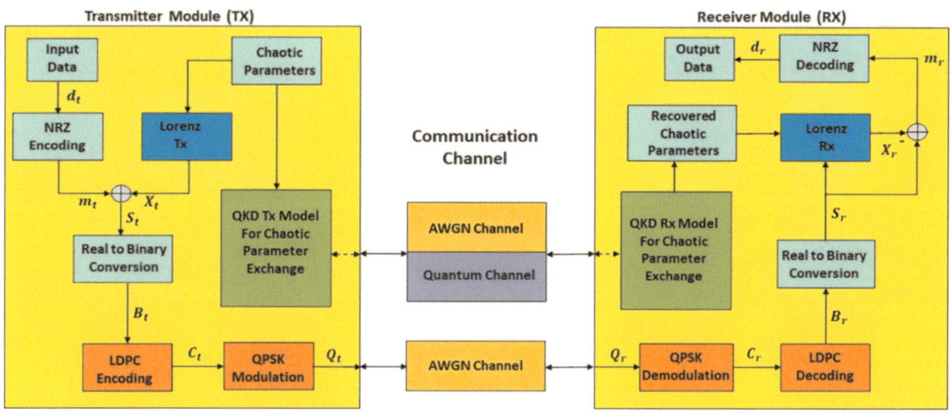

Figure 16.
Chaotic communication system secured by QKD [36].

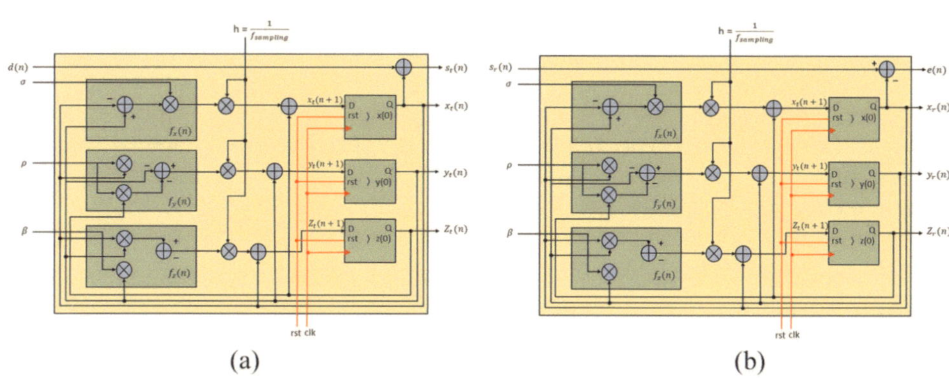

Figure 17.
The communication scheme's transmitter and receiver hardware models [36]. (a) Chaotic transmitter model. (b) Chaotic receiver model.

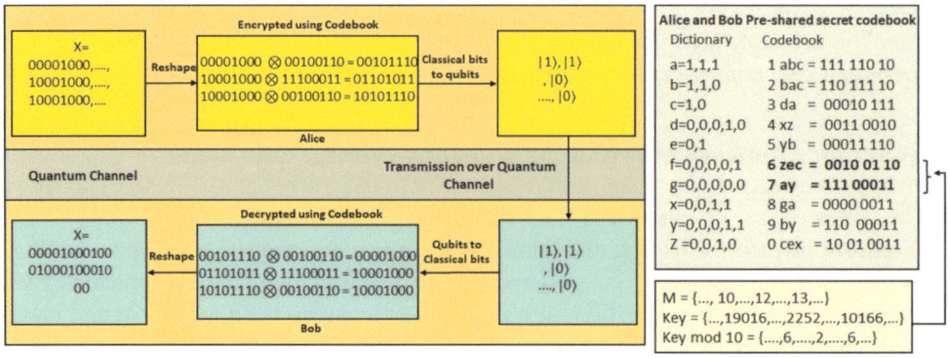

Figure 18.
Preshared codebook for encrypting/decrypting data [36].

(a) (b) (c)

Figure 19.
Transmission of a (512 × 512)-pixel image between Alice and Bob at SNR = 0.1dB, with interception attempted by Eve [36]. (a) Original image transmitted by Alice using parameters $\sigma = 10$, $\rho = 54$, $\beta = 4$. (b) Reconstructed image by Bob using recovered parameters $\sigma = 10$, $\rho = 54$, $\beta = 4$ and 0% pixel error. (c) Reconstructed image by Eve using incorrect parameters $\sigma = 10$, $\rho = 45.6$, $\beta = 14$ and 98.4652% pixel error.

central characters are defined as Alice (the sender or source of information), Bob (intended recipient), and Eve (eavesdropper seeking unauthorized access to transmitted data). The effectiveness of this technique is illustrated by the practical experimental results shown in **Figure 19**, please refer to [16] for complete results.
Figure 19b shows the grayscale image of size (512 × 512) pixels transmitted by Alice and reconstructed by Bob showing 0% error in pixels between the original and reconstructed image. However, when Eve tries to reconstruct the image without knowing the choatic parameters quantumly shared by Alice and Bob, it results in 98.46% pixel error, see **Figure 19c**.

6. Conclusions

The rapid advancement of quantum computing technology has opened up a realm of possibilities for practical applications of quantum computing. Throughout this chapter, a spectrum of these applications, including dimension reduction, pattern recognition, quantum sorting, and quantum communications were explored. This chapter presented optimized circuits for QWT to achieve efficient dimension reduction in multi-dimensional high-resolution data and an innovative approach for pattern recognition using QWT and Grover's search. For practical implementations of these algorithms, methodologies for classical-to-quantum (C2Q) data encoding and quantum-to-classical (Q2C) data decoding were also presented. This chapter also presented an efficient quantum sorting technique, which amalgamates perfect-shuffle and bitonic networks. Finally, in the field of quantum communications, a novel free-space optical (FSO) communication system that combines chaotic communications with Quantum Key Distribution (QKD) was discussed focusing on enhancing security and extending the communication range. This chapter serves as an invitation to readers to explore further, delve deeper, and engage with the ongoing journey of quantum computing's practical impact on various domains.

Acknowledgements

This research used resources of the Oak Ridge Leadership Computing Facility, which is a DOE Office of Science User Facility supported under Contract DE-AC05-00OR22725.

Nomenclature and abbreviations

QWT	quantum wavelet transform
QHT	quantum haar transform
C2Q	Classical-to-quantum
Q2C	quantum-to-classical
QKD	quantum-key-distribution
HPRC	high-performance-reconfigurable computers
NISQ	Noisy Intermediate Scale Quantum
QGS	multi-pattern Grover's search

Author details

Esam El-Araby*†, Manu Chaudhary†, Ishraq Ul Islam†, David Levy†, Dylan Kneidel†, Mingyoung Jeng†, Alvir Nobel† and Vinayak Jha†
The University of Kansas, Lawrence, USA

*Address all correspondence to: esam@ku.edu

† These authors contributed equally.

References

[1] Shor PW. Algorithms for quantum computation: Discrete logarithms and factoring. In: Proceedings 35th Annual Symposium on Foundations of Computer Science. New Mexico, USA: IEEE; 1994. pp. 124-134

[2] Bennett CH, DiVincenzo DP. Quantum information and computation. Nature. 2000;**404**(6775):247-255

[3] Preskill J. Quantum computing in the nisq era and beyond. Quantum. 2018;**2**:79

[4] Schlosshauer M. Quantum decoherence. Physics Reports. 2019;**831**: 1-57

[5] Zhang C, Chen Y, Jin Y, Ahn W, Zhang Y, Zhang EZ. A depth-aware swap insertion scheme for the qubit mapping problem. arXiv preprint arXiv: 2002.07289. 2020

[6] Shende VV, Bullock SS, Markov IL. Synthesis of quantum-logic circuits. IEEE Transactions on Computer-Aided Design of Integrated Circuits and Systems. 2006;**25**(6):1000-1010

[7] Mottonen M, Vartiainen JJ, Bergholm V, Salomaa MM. Transformation of quantum states using uniformly controlled rotations. arXiv preprint quant-ph/0407010. 2004

[8] Niemann P, Datta R, Wille R. Logic synthesis for quantum state generation. In: 2016 IEEE 46th International Symposium on Multiple-Valued Logic (ISMVL). Sapporo, Japan: IEEE; 2016. pp. 247-252

[9] Weigold M, Barzen J, Leymann F, Salm M. Data encoding patterns for quantum computing. In: Proceedings of the 27th Conference on Pattern Languages of Programs (online). 2020. pp. 1-11

[10] El-Araby E, Mahmud N, Jeng MJ, MacGillivray A, Manu Chaudhary M, Nobel AI, et al. Towards complete and scalable emulation of quantum algorithms on high-performance reconfigurable computers. IEEE Transactions on Computers. 2023;**72**(8): 2350-2364

[11] Williams CP. Explorations in Quantum Computing. Berlin, Germany: Springer Science & Business Media; 2010

[12] Mahmud N, Haase-Divine B, MacGillivray A, El-Araby E. Quantum dimension reduction for pattern recognition in high-resolution spatio-spectral data. IEEE Transactions on Computers. 2020;**71**(1):1-12

[13] El-Araby E, El-Ghazawi T, Le Moigne J, Gaj K. Wavelet spectral dimension reduction of hyperspectral imagery on a reconfigurable computer. In: Proceedings. 2004 IEEE International Conference on Field-Programmable Technology (IEEE Cat. No. 04EX921). Brisbane, Australia: IEEE; 2004. pp. 399-402

[14] Li H-S, Fan P, Xia H-y, Song S, He X. The multi-level and multi-dimensional quantum wavelet packet transforms. Scientific Reports. 2018;**8**(1):1-23

[15] Wickmann JMG. A Wavelet Approach to Dimension Reduction and Classification of Hyperspectral Data. [Thesis]. Faculty of Mathematics and Natural Sciences, University of Oslo. 2007

[16] Mahmud N, Macgillivray A, Chaudhary M, El-Araby E.

Decoherence-optimized circuits for multi-dimensional and multi-level decomposable quantum wavelet transform. IEEE Internet Computing (IEEE IC) Special Issue on Quantum and Post-Moore's Law Computing. 2022; **26**(1):15-25

[17] Mingyoung Jeng SM, Islam DL, Riachi A, Manu Chaudhary M, Nobel AI, Kneidel D, et al. Improving quantum-to-classical data decoding using optimized quantum wavelet transform. The Journal of Supercomputing. 2023;**2023**: 1-30

[18] Mahmud N, Jeng MJ, et al. Time-efficient quantum-to-classical data decoding. In: The International Conference on Emergent Quantum Technologies (ICEQT 2022). To appear in Transactions on Computational Science & Computational Intelligence. Las Vegas, Nevada, USA: Springer Nature – Research Book Series; 2022

[19] Imola K. A Survey of Dimension Reduction Techniques. California: Lawrence Livermore National Lab; 2002

[20] Mahmud N, El-Araby E. Dimension reduction for efficient pattern recognition in high spatial resolution data using quantum algorithms. In: 2019 32nd IEEE International System-on-Chip Conference (SOCC). California, USA: IEEE; 2019. pp. 126-131

[21] Lov K. A fast quantum mechanical algorithm for database search. In: Proceedings of the Twenty-eighth Annual ACM Symposium on Theory of Computing. Pennsylvania, USA. 1996. pp. 212-219

[22] Yanofsky NS, Mannucci MA. Quantum Computing for Computer Scientists. Cambridge, England: Cambridge University Press; 2008

[23] Mahmud N, Haase-Divine B, MacGillivray A, Srimoungchanh B, Kuhnke A, Blankenau N, et al. Modifying quantum grover's algorithm for dynamic multi-pattern search on reconfigurable hardware. Journal of Computational Electronics. 2020;**19**:1215-1231

[24] Boyer M, Brassard G, Høyer P, Tapp A. Tight bounds on quantum searching. Fortschritte der Physik: Progress of Physics. 1998;**46**(4–5):493-505

[25] Mahmud N, Srimoungchanh B, Haase-Divine B, Blankenau N, Kuhnke A, El-Araby E. Combining perfect shuffle and bitonic networks for efficient quantum sorting. In: 2019 IEEE/ ACM International Workshop on Heterogeneous High-Performance Reconfigurable Computing (H2RC). Denver, CO, USA: IEEE; 2019. pp. 42-49

[26] Akl SG. Parallel Sorting Algorithms. Vol. 12. Cambridge, Massachusetts: Academic Press; 2014

[27] Kenneth E. Sorting networks and their applications. In: Proceedings of the April 30–May 2, 1968. Spring Joint Computer Conference. New York, NY, USA. 1968. pp. 307-314

[28] Stone HS. Parallel processing with the perfect shuffle. IEEE Transactions on Computers. 1971;**100**(2):153-161

[29] Guan W, Perdue G, Pesah A, Schuld M, Terashi K, Vallecorsa S, et al. Quantum machine learning in high energy physics. Machine Learning: Science and Technology. 2021;**2**(1): 011003

[30] Weigold M, Barzen J, Leymann F, Salm M. Data encoding patterns for quantum computing. In: HILLSIDE Proceedings of Conference on Pattern Languages of Programs'22. Portland, Oregon, USA. 2020

[31] Lanzagorta M, Uhlmann J. Is quantum parallelism real? In: Quantum Information and Computation VI. Vol. 6976. Bellingham, WA, USA: International Society for Optics and Photonics; 2008. p. 69760W

[32] Pecora LM, Carroll TL. Synchronization in chaotic systems. Physical Review Letters. 1990;**64**(8):821

[33] Lorenz EN. Deterministic nonperiodic flow. Journal of Atmospheric Sciences. 1963;**20**(2): 130-141

[34] Shor PW, Preskill J. Simple proof of security of the bb84 quantum key distribution protocol. Physical Review Letters. 2000;**85**(2):441

[35] Bennett CH, Brassard G. Quantum cryptography: Public key distribution and coin tossing. *arXiv preprint arXiv: 2003.06557*. 2020

[36] Mahmud N, MacGillivray A, Rai A, Patterson J, Gharaibeh A, El-Araby E, et al. Combining quantum key distribution with chaotic systems for free-space optical communications. Quantum Information Processing. 2021; **20**:1-25